Jane-Anne Hobbs

Scrumptious

FOOD FOR FAMILY AND FRIENDS

Jane-Anne Hobbs

Jane-Anne Hobbs
Scrumptious
FOOD FOR FAMILY AND FRIENDS

Photography by Michael Le Grange

MY THANKS TO …

Random House Struik's dream team: Publisher Linda de Villiers, for her passion and acumen; book designer Beverley Dodd, for her brilliant art direction and humour; Joy Clack for her keen-eyed, sensitive editing. Photographer and master of light Michael Le Grange: working with you was a privilege, Dicky. Master potter of Franschhoek David Walters, my uncle, who hand-made the exquisite porcelain plates, platters and bowls: our collaboration has been a joy, Dave. Queen of South African cookery writers Lynn Bedford Hall, for so graciously agreeing to write the foreword. My wonderful mother Jenny Hobbs, for her boundless enthusiasm and clever editing. For support, generosity and sharing recipes: Margie and Bertrand Vidal, Sarah Dall, Judy Levy, Claire Robertson, Tracey Hawthorne, Kaylah Greenberg, Cecilia Barfield, Michael Olivier, Adrienne Verlaque-Napper, Nina Timm, Roz Berzen, Gilly Walters, Michelle Walters, Steve Mabbutt, Michael Karamanof, Pieter van Niekerk, Christopher Duigan, Cindy McKenzie and James Robertson. Most of all, my family: Flip, Luke, Tristan and Ellie. I love you with all my heart. Thanks for being so honest about my food.

JANE-ANNE HOBBS

Twitter hashtag: #ScrumptiousFood

Published in 2012 by Struik Lifestyle
(an imprint of Random House Struik (Pty) Ltd)
Company Reg. No. 1966/003153/07
Wembley Square, 1st Floor, Solan Street, Gardens 8001
P O Box 1144, Cape Town 8000

Visit **www.randomstruik.co.za** and subscribe to our newsletter for monthly updates and news.

Publisher: Linda de Villiers
Managing editor: Cecilia Barfield
Editor and indexer: Joy Clack
Designer: Beverley Dodd
Photographer: Michael Le Grange
Food stylist: Jane-Anne Hobbs
Food preparation: Sarah Dall
Proofreader: Bronwen Leak

Reproduction: Hirt & Carter Cape (Pty) Ltd
Printing and binding: Craft Print International Ltd, Singapore

The fine porcelain tableware in the photographs courtesy of master potter David Walters (www.davidwalters.co.za).

Contents

Foreword

When you are asked to write the foreword to a book, you cannot do so without first perusing the page proofs. Which I did. For hours and hours. After which my tastebuds were tingling with such a pot-pourri of flavours, and I was so hungry that I needed to go for a long walk to sort out my culinary opinions. The walk lasted 5 minutes – round the block, in fact, before I found myself back in the kitchen, making shopping lists, staking out recipes, and then standing back in astonishment at how someone who is not only an editor, a journalist, a foodwriter, a published author AND a time-strapped mother of three could produce a book such as this: a cookbook which is not simply a last-minute scurry of quick 'n easy recipes. On the contrary, *Scrumptious* is a book which encourages home cooks to cook with care and patience, to focus on flavour, pay attention to detail, and to bin all thoughts of twirls and towers to dolly up the dish. Taste, here, is paramount.

Reading these pages is an entertainment in itself. Jane-Anne's text and descriptions bounce with her singular turns of phrase; her detailed instructions take the fright out of trying an unfamiliar dish; and the plethora of tips she offers will prepare both the novice and the experienced cook for an adventure into serious, good cooking which should not intimidate, because she helps you every step of the way because – as I said – she *can* cook, she will not countenance second best – and she understands you. A big plus is that this book inspires confidence. When you read 'one slice of lemon, no more'; or '8–10 strands of saffron, no more'; 'refrigerate at this point'; 'assemble now'; 'prepare 2 hours ahead'; when you read precise instructions like these, you are instantly relieved of anxiously fumbling with your own decisions.

Another plus is the author's disarming honesty. She will warn you when a dish contains an 'indecent amount of Cheddar', or a 'scandalous quantity of butter', and she certainly is not shy with cream or pricey Parmesan. Therefore, if you are contemplating a fine dining event, the caviar is there between the pages; also the Parma ham; the fillets and the seafood. The family, however, is not forgotten. Turn the pages and you'll also find sosaties and ginger sponge, cheesecake and fruit popsicles. It's an eclectic book and it travels all over as the author explores international cuisines – French, Italian, Moroccan, Russian … which means you might have to trawl the suburbs for certain ingredients, but most are probably already at home in your pantry or fridge. Except, perhaps, for her 'Figs With Hot Brie and Caramel Walnuts' (just imagine that!), but you will definitely be able to replicate, for example, the bright version of Coronation Chicken. The photographs throughout are just brilliant.

Jane-Anne's *Scrumptious* certainly lives up to its name.

Lynn Bedford Hall

Introduction

Food is all about celebrating life, love and friendship, isn't it? Think back on some of the happiest moments of your life, and chances are you'll recall sitting at a table surrounded by people you love. The meals your mum or dad or grandma made for you may not have been sophisticated by modern standards, but they linger in your memory for a very long time because they tasted like home and happiness.

I wouldn't dream of eating porridge with peanut butter as an adult, but I have wonderful memories of sitting in a sunny kitchen with a bunch of friends, laughing until my sides hurt and tucking into a bowl of hot Jungle Oats with cold, thick cream and a dollop of sticky peanut butter. And of eating sizzling, spicy boerewors hot off the braai, from a paper plate, with a sunburned nose and the sounds of crashing surf filtering through a grove of milkwood trees. And falling like a starving wolf onto a plate of bangers, mash and tomato gravy, which tasted like heaven to me even though it had been slumbering under a sheet of foil for several hours by the time I got home from school. These were the plainest of dishes, yet they made me feel both happy and loved, and it is this – putting comfort and joy together on a plate – that seems to me the very essence of good home cooking.

And that is why this book is about creating memorable meals for the people you love.

How do you create a meal that delivers a wallop of flavour, arrives at the table fresh, piping hot and on time, and is cooked to perfection? This may seem like a tall order if you haven't much time on your hands, or you don't feel very confident in the kitchen. Whether you're catering for a special-occasion feast or a more intimate family gathering, the same principles apply: passion, planning, preparation, patience and practice. Of the five, planning and preparation are by far the most important. If you plan a meal carefully, pay close attention to crucial details and prepare as much as you can in advance, you can sail to the table with your head held high, confident in the knowledge that you've left nothing to chance. With all your proverbial ducks in a row, you'll be able to spend the meal eating, drinking and making merry with your guests (not footsore and cursing in the kitchen, vowing never to throw a dinner party again).

This advice may sound rather obvious if you're someone who plans a party like a military campaign, but I think it's worth repeating because it's so easy to lose sight of just how much painstaking behind-the-scenes work goes into producing a meal of exceptional quality. We're bombarded with seductive recipes from a host of television shows, magazines, books and blogs, and so often they make good cookery seem effortless when in fact it is quite the opposite. As interest in cookery has surged worldwide over the past decade, so cooking has become a competitive sport, and one where the rules change all the time. It's not good enough to put a plain roast chicken and some rustling golden spuds on the table: it has to be a free-range organic chicken, with heirloom potatoes sourced from the farmer next door, and if your bird hasn't been brined and basted and barded you might as well throw the lot in the bin, and send your sorry old box of gravy powder after it.

Paradoxically, and hand in hand with the rise of foodier-than-thou elitism, we are exhorted to do everything faster: best you'd put a three-course masterpiece on the table in under 30 minutes or off to the naughty step you go. I'm not quibbling with quick, clever recipes – time is a luxury and few of us have it – but what riles me is that there's so much emphasis on speed and so little on thoughtful, patient cooking. What's more, I worry that young people who've learned how to cook by watching reality TV (as opposed to soaking up knowledge at the elbow of a grandmother, or by reading books) are missing out on learning much of the craftsmanship that underpins great home cooking.

I don't mean to belittle celebrity cooks or reality TV shows (anyone who encourages people to cook good food at home is a hero in my eyes), but I think that it's worth pointing out that what you see isn't always what you taste. The final dish, by the time it appears on a screen or page, has been tweaked and freshened – or made all over again for that perfect, glistening shot – by a professional food stylist. And because of the time restrictions of television, finer details of the cooking process are, by necessity, edited out, but it is these small but vital steps that often make all the difference to the end result. This is misleading at best and dishonest at worst, and certainly not doing budding home cooks any favours. A disappointing result can undermine your confidence as a cook, and leave you feeling resentful about the money you've wasted on good ingredients. Even worse: there's a possibility that this sort of quick, slapdash cooking may engender a sense of false confidence in young cooks, and leave them thinking their food's so damned awesome that there's no need to try harder.

Trying harder doesn't mean producing fussy, complicated food, or using expensive ingredients, or coming up with daring flavour combinations. The best home-cooked food is all about simplicity, freshness and flavour; it's honest food, cooked with love, generosity and an open heart. This may be difficult to believe, but many chefs working in pressurised restaurant kitchens can think of nothing nicer than being invited to a relaxed meal at a friend's home. 'People never ask me to dinner,' a top chef complained to me recently. 'They say they're too intimidated to cook for me. But all I really want is some plain home cooking.' You may not rate your own cooking very highly, but I can promise you that there are many professional chefs who long to climb into a nutmeggy homemade chicken pie, or a shimmering vegetable broth, or your grandma's boozy tinned-peach trifle.

In this book, I've come up with a selection of recipes that I think are ideal for relaxed home entertaining. My recipes have modern elements, reflecting new ingredients and trends in food, but you will also find many dishes that express a yearning nostalgia for the food I enjoyed as a child. I've developed many of the recipes from scratch; others are a new twist on classic recipes from the past. I haven't paid any attention to calories, because special-occasion meals are all about indulgence. Not piggery or extravagance, mind you: because I'm minding a household budget, I endeavour to use humble and inexpensive ingredients in my dishes where possible, and then place a jaunty feather in their hats by finishing off with a small quantity of something luxurious: a drizzle of white-truffle oil, a few spoonfuls of caviar, a splash of excellent liqueur …

Here are ten things worth considering when you want to create a truly scrumptious feast:

Keep it simple: It takes confidence to pull together a dish that has few ingredients, but if they are fresh and of good quality, and you've prepared them with care, the end result will always be sensational. This is not to say that you should restrict yourself to only four or five ingredients, but it's worth remembering that the real test of a good cook is weaving just a few basic notes into a joyful orchestra of flavour.

Create complex flavours: This may seem to contradict my 'keep it simple' advice above, but creating intriguing layers of flavour is one of the cornerstones of good home cooking. Homemade stocks, judicious spicing and careful, slow cooking all help to produce good depth of flavour.

Balance and harmony: An excellent dish comprises a pleasing balance of flavours, and its component ingredients work together seamlessly, like a company of ballet dancers. There's always the prima ballerina – the starring ingredient in the dish – but everything else on the plate is there to support her. If your main course is lamb, let the lamb shine, and choose as accompaniments ingredients that have a natural affinity with this meat: rosemary, mint, garlic, lemons, aubergines, and so on. Stick to simple, clean, well-defined flavours that work harmoniously together.

Contrast and texture: A really satisfying dish contains interesting contrasts, such as creamy and crunchy, sweet and sour, mild and peppery, hot and cold, and so on. Don't overlook the importance of texture: even the most humble vegetable soup, for example, can achieve greatness with a topping of crisp, crumbled bacon or a handful of garlicky croutons.

Tasting and measuring: I often hear people say, 'Oh, I don't follow recipes. I just add a little bit of this and a little bit of that, and make it up as I go along.' This is all very well if you're an accomplished cook with a good palate, but there's no better way to learn how flavours go together than carefully following well-thought-out recipes. Measuring accurately is very important too: many a good dish is ruined by a heavy hand with one aggressive ingredient – honey, saffron, passion fruit, rocket, balsamic vinegar, rosemary, fish sauce, cardamom and cumin, to name just a few. This is not to say that there isn't room for improvement in any recipe, or that you shouldn't feel free to adapt it to your liking, but it's always a good idea to measure first, then keep tasting and adding until you're satisfied with the result.

Follow your heart: When you're planning a menu, choose food that you like, that strikes a chord in your heart and that you eat often. If you like a dish, the chances are that your friends will love it too. But, at the same time, avoid food that may have a 'yuck' factor, especially to people you don't know well: bony whole fish, for example, or tripe, kidneys and other sorts of offal. Avoid faddish ingredients and be wary of trendy techniques: dots and dabs and clouds of foam are all very well in a restaurant, but they add little to a plate of lovely home-cooked food.

Prepare ahead: I don't think you should spend more than 5–10 minutes per course in the kitchen attending to last-minute cooking details, and this is quite achievable if you start your preparations well ahead of time. In most of the recipes in this book I've indicated which elements of the dish can be prepared beforehand without suffering any loss of flavour or texture. Make stocks, sauces, soups and stews a day or two in advance, whip up puddings the night before, and line up all your serving platters, spoons and jugs on a sideboard. Don't overlook the time it takes to organise the finer details of entertaining: sparkling glasses and cutlery, clean napery, iced water, fresh flowers and candles, and – last but not least – a spotless bathroom.

Clean as you go, and be methodical: Take a tip from chefs in top professional kitchens and adopt a laboratory approach to your workspace. This means wiping down counters and boards and washing dirty utensils immediately after you finish each stage of preparation. Line up all your ingredients and utensils before you start cooking. This methodical approach will not stifle your creativity: in fact, the very opposite applies. Because you're not hindered by piles of dishes, or scrabbling to find the right utensil, or fighting a sinking heart as the kitchen turns into a bombsite, you'll be able to pour all your concentration into preparing food with real flair.

Stay calm and focused: If your feet are sore, or you're feeling tired and harassed, or people and animals are bouncing around your kitchen, you will not achieve the calm, focused right-brain state that careful cooking requires. Long experience has taught me that I turn out the best food when I'm in a serene and happy frame of mind. Constant interruptions will curdle your sauces and scorch your onions, so chase everyone out of the kitchen, switch off your phone and relax into the cooking process. I often cook very early in the morning (or late at night) before a special meal, because that's when the house is quietest.

Finesse and attention to detail: I have found that having a light touch with food makes an appreciable difference to its taste and appearance: watch top-notch chefs in action and you'll notice how delicately and carefully they handle ingredients. Whisk your sauces gently, handle pastry with tender fingers, chop your ingredients with care and precision, and you'll be rewarded with a finished dish that looks and tastes like the work of a professional.

Starters

A starter is a drumroll, a clapping of hands, a flourish of trumpets to lift the curtains on a splendid meal. Whether you're serving a formal first course or a selection of interesting nibbles to go with drinks (my family calls these 'little snacky things'), this is your chance to sparkle and shine from the moment your guests arrive, hungry and ready to party.

A good first course fires the taste buds, gets the conversation rolling and hints at delicious things to come. Freshness, knock-out flavours and simplicity are the keys to creating a great curtain-raiser for a home feast. A starter should never be an attention-seeking strumpet of a dish: fiddly, fussy food is best left to chefs slaving in restaurant kitchens.

Starters and snacks should be served in modest portions — though by modest, I don't mean stingy. Servings must be just enough to whet the appetite, but not so generous that everyone's too stuffed to enjoy anticipating the next course. Most of the recipes in this chapter provide three to four good mouthfuls per person, which I think is quite sufficient if there's a huge banquet to follow, but if you're expecting a team of champion eaters, make two or three different snacks, or put a few loaves of warm bread on the table, with some butter, and a bowl of olive oil for dipping.

You might choose to have no warm-up course at all, but I wouldn't recommend it. One of the crucial roles of a starter is to armour-plate your innards against the wine that is quaffed (with good reason) at a memorable feast. My father always insisted that a drink in our house should be accompanied by a snack, even if it was a humble slice of warm homemade wholewheat bread with cold butter, pickled onions and Cheddar (in fact, it was almost always exactly that).

The best starters and snacks, I think, are those placed on big communal platters in the middle of the table. When dinner parties were all the rage during the Eighties, I spent many anxious minutes plating up fiddly little towers of this and nests of that. Now I concentrate on creating one or two simple but embracing dishes that everyone will enjoy tucking into. The whole essence of a feast is that it's a happy, communal meal, so the more reaching, sharing and finger-licking that goes on, the better.

You'll find more ideas for salad and soup starters on pp. 25–51.

Smoked Venison with Cream Cheese and Horseradish

Paper-thin smoked venison, fresh horseradish, cream cheese and white pepper, all brought together with a tart, sweet pomegranate syrup.

2 x 250 g tubs full-fat cream cheese
4 tsp (20 ml) peeled and very finely grated fresh horseradish or 5 tsp (25 ml) bottled creamed horseradish
1 tsp (5 ml) white pepper
4 tsp (20 ml) olive oil
salt, to taste
12 paper-thin slices smoked venison
2 Tbsp (30 ml) pomegranate syrup
pomegranate seeds or baby herb leaves

Mix the cream cheese, horseradish and white pepper in a bowl, adding just enough olive oil to create a rather stiff, smooth mixture. Season with salt. Lightly oil two small bowls and press a sheet of clingfilm into each. Line the bowls with venison, overlapping the edges by a few centimetres. Pack the cream cheese mixture into the moulds, smooth the tops and fold the overlapping pieces of venison over the filling. Cover and chill for 2 hours. Unmould onto two plates and remove the clingfilm. Trickle pomegranate syrup onto the plate, around the venison moulds, and top with pomegranate seeds or herbs. Serve with crackers or melba toast.

Serves 8 as a snack.

Notes

Make up to 8 hours in advance, but pour on the syrup at the last minute. Pomegranate syrup is available at delicatessens.

Happy Piglets with Whipped Mustard Sauce

My family's Christmas feasts always include these (photo, p. 10). Nobody would care if we cancelled the turkey, but the sausages are compulsory.

16 rashers streaky bacon, halved crossways
32 pork chipolatas
fresh rosemary sprigs

Heat the oven to 180 °C. Wrap the bacon rashers around the sausages and tuck a small rosemary sprig into each. Place on a non-stick baking sheet and bake for 20–30 minutes, or until the sausages are cooked and the bacon crisp.

FOR THE SAUCE
5 Tbsp (75 ml) white wine vinegar
½ onion, peeled and finely chopped
1 tsp (5 ml) dried tarragon
3 egg yolks
2 Tbsp (30 ml) water
1½ tsp (7.5 ml) hot English mustard powder
4 Tbsp (60 ml) Dijon mustard
1 Tbsp (15 ml) butter
salt and milled black pepper
175 ml cream, whipped to a soft peak

For the sauce, simmer the vinegar, onion and tarragon in a small saucepan for 4–5 minutes, or until reduced by half. Put the egg yolks, water, mustard powder, Dijon mustard and butter into a metal or glass bowl and whisk until creamy. Strain the warm vinegar onto the eggs and mix well. Put the bowl over a pan of simmering water and cook, whisking constantly, for 4–5 minutes, or until hot and very thick. Do not allow to boil. Season to taste, cool for 3 minutes, and then fold in the whipped cream. Chill.

Serve the sausages hot with the cold mustard sauce.

Serves 8 as a snack.

Double-Craggy Garlic and Herb Bread with Peppered Cheese

I've updated this great classic by cutting the bread into stalagmites and crumbling over it some peppery cheese.

1 large round loaf of bread or 2 smaller ones, a day or two old
1½ cups (375 ml) melted butter
10 cloves garlic, peeled and finely grated
finely grated zest of 1 lemon
½ cup (125 ml) chopped fresh herbs
milled black pepper
200 g peppered feta cheese, goat's cheese or crumbly cream cheese

Heat the oven to 190 °C. Using a sharp serrated knife, cut the bread into 2-cm slices, to within 2 cm of its base. Now turn the loaf the other way and, using quick, light sawing motions, cut across the slices to form a grid. Mix together the melted butter, garlic, lemon zest, fresh herbs and pepper. Gently squeeze the base of the loaf to splay the crags and, using a brush or a baster, coat each one with flavoured butter. Brush the bread all over with more melted butter and tie a piece of damp string or raffia around its middle. Cover with foil and bake for 10 minutes. Remove the foil and bake for a further 10 minutes, or until the bread is golden brown and crisp. Crumble over the cheese and bake for a further 5 minutes. Remove the string and serve hot.

Serves 8 as a snack.

Notes	Add anything you fancy to the melted butter: dried chilli flakes, pounded anchovies, finely chopped olives, grated Parmesan, and so on. Prepare the garlic bread for baking up to 24 hours ahead.

Mashed Feta with Artichokes, Lemon and Olive Oil

This zingy, creamy dip is such a versatile dish because it can be served at room temperature in summer or piping hot and molten in winter. The chilli flakes add a lovely freckling of scarlet, but leave them out if there are children at the table.

3 wheels (about 240 g) feta cheese, drained
1 x 400 g tin artichoke hearts, drained and chopped
2 Tbsp (30 ml) olive oil
4 Tbsp (60 ml) sour cream
1 clove garlic, peeled and finely grated
juice and finely grated zest of 1 lemon
salt and milled black pepper
extra olive oil, for drizzling
2 Tbsp (30 ml) chopped fresh flat-leaf parsley
½ tsp (2.5 ml) dried chilli flakes, or to taste

Crumble the feta into a bowl and add the artichokes, olive oil, sour cream, garlic and lemon juice and zest. Using a fork, mash the mixture to form a slightly chunky paste. Season with salt and pepper. If you're serving the dip cold, pile it into a shallow bowl, drizzle over 3 Tbsp (45 ml) olive oil and sprinkle with parsley and chilli flakes. If you're serving it hot, pack it into two small ovenproof dishes and bake at 180 °C for 10–15 minutes, or until hot and bubbling. Top with olive oil, parsley and chilli flakes, and serve immediately. Good with toasted pita bread or crudités.

Serves 8 as a snack.

Silken Tuna Pâté with Green Peppercorns

Lemony tuna pâté was all the rage in the Seventies, and I think it's time to revive this classic. Here, I've whizzed it absolutely smooth with a lot of butter and given it a kick with brined green peppercorns and Italian white anchovy fillets.

2 x 170 g tins tuna in oil, drained
100 g (100 ml) very soft butter
1 Tbsp (15 ml) olive oil
4 Tbsp (60 ml) sour cream
1½ tsp (7.5 ml) finely grated lemon zest
2 Tbsp (30 ml) freshly squeezed lemon juice
5 Italian white anchovies (optional)
salt and milled black pepper
5 tsp (25 ml) brined green peppercorns, drained
6 large slices smoked salmon

Put the tuna, butter, olive oil, sour cream, lemon zest and juice into a blender and process to a smooth, silken paste. If the blades are reluctant to turn, add a few drops of warm water. Whizz in the anchovies if you're using them. Lightly crush the peppercorns with a rolling pin and stir them into the pâté. Season to taste. Lightly oil two small bowls and press a sheet of clingfilm into each. Line the bowls with the smoked salmon, allowing the slices to overlap the edges by a few centimetres. Pack the pâté into the moulds, smooth off the tops and fold the overlapping pieces of salmon back over the filling. Cover and chill for 2 hours. Unmould onto two serving plates and peel away the clingfilm. Serve with crackers or triangles of hot toast.

Serves 8 as a snack.

Warm White-Bean Purée with Garlic and Tahina

This easy dip (photo, p. 10) is essentially a hummus, but it has a silkier texture and is marvellously fragrant because the heat of the beans releases the flavours of the garlic, lemon and cumin.

2 x 400 g tins white beans, drained
1 cup (250 ml) water
1 thin slice of lemon, peel on
100 ml extra-virgin olive oil, plus a little extra
7 tsp (35 ml) freshly squeezed lemon juice
1 Tbsp (15 ml) raw tahina
1 tsp (5 ml) ground cumin
1 clove garlic, peeled and chopped
salt and milled black pepper
4 Tbsp (60 ml) pine nuts, lightly toasted
1 tsp (5 ml) chilli powder or cayenne pepper
3 Tbsp (45 ml) chopped fresh flat-leaf parsley

Put the beans, water and slice of lemon in a saucepan and bring to the boil. Simmer briskly for 10 minutes, or until almost all the liquid has evaporated. Tip the hot beans into a blender, add the oil, lemon juice, tahina, cumin and garlic and whizz until smooth and silken. If the blades are reluctant to turn, add a little warm water. Season with salt and pepper. Tip the purée into two warmed serving bowls and, using a teaspoon, draw a deep swirl over the surfaces. Drizzle with a little extra olive oil and sprinkle with the toasted pine nuts, chilli powder and parsley. Serve immediately with crackers, crisps or crudités.

Serves 8 as a snack.

Notes

To prepare ahead, cook the beans until just a little liquid remains, and then cover. Prepare all the remaining dip ingredients and place them ready in the liquidiser. When it's time to serve, reheat the beans and continue with the recipe.

Peri-Peri Calamari with Chouriço Sausage

Peri-peri is one of South Africa's favourite flavours, and here I've used this delicious Afro-Portuguese sauce to set fire to tender tubes of calamari. Feel free to add more fresh chillies if you appreciate a blisteringly hot sauce.

800 g calamari tubes and tentacles, cleaned
2 litres boiling water
3 Tbsp (45 ml) olive oil
1 large chouriço sausage, skinned
3 cloves garlic, peeled and finely chopped
salt and milled black pepper
½ cup (125 ml) chopped fresh parsley
8 lemon wedges, to serve

FOR THE DRESSING
2 large dried bay leaves
1 tsp (5 ml) sea salt flakes
juice and finely grated zest of 2 lemons
2 tsp (10 ml) chilli oil
1 tsp (5 ml) chilli powder
1 fresh red chilli, deseeded and finely chopped
1½ tsp (7.5 ml) paprika

First make the dressing. Use a mortar and pestle to pound the bay leaves and salt to a coarse powder. Add the remaining dressing ingredients and stir well to combine.

Cut along the long sides of the calamari tubes and spread flat. Scrape away the membranes and score the inner side of the flesh into a diamond pattern, using the tip of a sharp knife. (If the tubes are very small, leave them whole.) Fill a large bowl with the just-boiled water. Drop the tubes and tentacles into the water, leave for 1 minute, drain, and pat quite dry with kitchen paper. Heat 2 Tbsp (30 ml) of the olive oil in a frying pan set over a medium-high heat. Crumble half the chouriço sausage and finely slice the other half. Sizzle the chouriço pieces in the hot oil for a minute or two, or until lightly browned. Remove from the pan and drain on kitchen paper. Turn the heat under the pan to its maximum and fry the calamari tubes and tentacles, in small batches, for 1½ minutes, but no longer. Tip the calamari into a mixing bowl. Wipe out the frying pan, add another tablespoon of oil, turn down the heat and gently fry the garlic for 1 minute, without allowing it to brown. Pour in the prepared dressing and bubble, over a low heat, for another minute. Tip the calamari and sausage bits back into the pan, turn up the heat, and cook for a further minute, or until heated right through. Season with pepper and more salt, if necessary.

Tip the calamari onto a heated platter. Scatter with chopped parsley and serve hot, with lemon wedges and crusty bread.

Serves 8 as a snack.

Notes

This is best with small, tender tubes of Patagonian calamari, available from fishmongers. Try to find an authentic chouriço sausage (or a Spanish chorizo) from a good deli. Clean the calamari, dice the ingredients and make the dressing up to 8 hours ahead, but cook the calamari at the last minute. Don't overcook the calamari: it turns to leather in an instant.

Ricotta and Chive Hotcakes with Smoked Salmon Twirls

A crisp delicate crust and a hot oozy filling make these little hotcakes a real crowd-pleaser. They are good warm but best served piping hot, so if you have a portable gas burner, make them at the table and let your guests help themselves to the toppings.

500 g fresh ricotta cheese
5 Tbsp (75 ml) finely grated Parmesan
2 extra-large eggs, separated
½ cup (125 ml) milk
½ cup (125 ml) cake flour
½ tsp (2.5 ml) baking powder
½ tsp (2.5 ml) salt
4 tsp (20 ml) finely snipped fresh chives
milled black pepper
sunflower oil for frying

TO SERVE
400 g finely sliced smoked salmon or trout
lemon wedges
milled black pepper
1 x 250 g tub crème fraîche or sour cream
caviar and capers (optional)

First make the salmon twirls. Cut the salmon slices into long strips about 2 cm wide. Twirl each slice into a loose spiral, place on a plate, cover with clingfilm and refrigerate. You'll need about 24.

Put the ricotta, Parmesan, egg yolks and milk into a large bowl and beat energetically with a wire whisk. Sift in the flour, baking powder and salt and mix to a batter. Stir in the chives and season with pepper. Using a clean whisk and bowl, beat the egg whites until stiff (but not dry), then gently fold them into the mixture. Heat 1 Tbsp (15 ml) oil in a large non-stick frying pan. Drop tablespoons of the batter into the pan and cook for 1 minute, or until the bottom edges turn golden brown. Flip over and cook for another minute, or until the hotcakes are puffed and their edges look set. Watch them like a hawk as they burn quickly. Keep warm.

Arrange the hotcakes on a platter and top each with a salmon twirl. Serve immediately with lemon wedges, black pepper and little bowls of crème fraîche, capers and caviar.

Makes about 24; serves 8 as a snack.

Notes

Prepare the salmon twirls up to 10 hours in advance and keep covered in the fridge. The batter can be made up to 6 hours in advance, but beat and fold in the egg whites just before you fry the hotcakes.

Seared Fillet Steak 'Carpaccio' with Thai-Style Dressing

It's impossible to produce paper-thin slices of carpaccio at home unless you have an industrial slicing machine, or you freeze the fillet first. I don't have the former and won't ruin the texture of the meat by doing the latter, so here's my solution – with a lovely zippy Asian dressing.

750 g fillet steak
a little olive oil
milled black pepper
2 Tbsp (30 ml) sunflower oil
sprouts for garnishing

FOR THE DRESSING
2 limes
1 Tbsp (15 ml) white sugar
5-cm piece of lemongrass, peeled and sliced
1 Tbsp (15 ml) grated fresh ginger
1 clove garlic, peeled and chopped
1 green chilli, deseeded and sliced
2 Tbsp (30 ml) sunflower oil
1 tsp (5 ml) finely grated palm sugar or brown sugar
1 tsp (5 ml) soy sauce
1 tsp (5 ml) fish sauce
2 tsp (10 ml) water
2 drops sesame oil

Rub a little olive oil all over the fillet and sprinkle generously with black pepper. Wrap the fillet lengthways in a large sheet of clingfilm and twist the ends to create a tight Christmas-cracker shape. Tuck the ends underneath and chill for at least 2 hours. Heat the oil in a large pan and, when extremely hot (but not smoking), quickly brown the meat on all sides. This should take no more than 3 minutes and the meat should remain quite raw inside. Set aside to cool for 10 minutes. Cut the fillet into slices about 5 mm thick. Place each slice between two sheets of clingfilm and use a rolling pin to thin and gently stretch the meat to the desired thickness.

To make the dressing, cut the limes in half and dip the cut end in the white sugar. Place them, sugar-side down, in a hot non-stick frying pan. Cook until the cut surface is nicely browned and caramelised. Cool for a few minutes, then squeeze the warm lime juice into the goblet of a blender. Add all the remaining dressing ingredients and whizz at high speed until well combined. Spread a little dressing on the base of a platter or several smaller plates. Arrange the carpaccio slices on top and drizzle with the remaining dressing. Garnish and serve immediately.

Serves 8 as a snack.

Notes: The fillet can be seared, sliced and refrigerated, and the dressing made, up to 3 hours in advance, but put them together just before you serve the dish or the dressing will 'cook' the fillet. If you can't find fresh limes, use lemons instead.

Salads

Salads have become simpler, lighter and fresher over the past two decades, and I'm certainly not complaining. My idea of a perfect salad is peppery rocket, watercress and baby spinach sparingly dressed with lemon juice, olive oil, salt and shavings of Parmesan, and I make sure there is a giant bowl of this on the table at every feast in my house.

A lavish meal needs at least one very plain salad, I think, even if it's a single, beautiful seasonal ingredient drizzled with a simple dressing designed to enhance, not overwhelm, its freshness and flavour.

Still, there is something to be said for the extravaganzas that were so popular when salads came of age during the health-food revolution of the late Seventies and early Eighties. When I was a teen, a salad was a square meal, a veritable salmagundi of dozens of ingredients: all the usual crunchy greens, plus cubed cheese, avocado, nuts, seeds, sprouts, peas, mushrooms, carrots, tomato wedges, tuna, olives, onion rings, boiled potatoes, and so on. And if that wasn't enough, the whole thing was topped off with croutons, crumbled bacon, parsley, chives, super-garlicky vinaigrettes and splodges of homemade mayonnaise.

It's easy to poke fun at this sort of over-eager salad now, but I remain a fan of composite salads, those generous meals-in-one that you can dish up in gigantic portions to a hungry crowd. They're versatile, abundant and fresh, and there's something in them for everyone.

So, in this chapter, I've given you some composite salads that can stand on their own as one-bowl meals. Some of these contain meat or fish, so if you're expecting vegetarian guests, put aside a portion of the salad or dressing before you add any meaty ingredients.

Unless otherwise specified, all these salads serve eight as a starter or side salad. If you want to serve these as a meal-in-one, perhaps with some nice bread or boiled potatoes, double the quantities.

Herb and Rice Salad with Feta, Walnuts and Broccoli Crumbs

It's a pity that old-fashioned rice salads have fallen out of favour, because these are versatile crowd-pleasers that allow you merrily to ring the changes with all sorts of interesting ingredients. This salad features some delicious flavours of the eastern Mediterranean: punchy herbs for freshness, walnuts for crunch, feta for creaminess and pomegranate seeds and sumac for an interesting 'ping!'. I've used plain rice, but this is also good with couscous, quinoa, bulgur wheat or a brown/wild rice combination.

2½ cups (625 ml) uncooked long-grain white rice
1 tsp (5 ml) salt
6 cups (1.5 litres) cold water
1 cup (250 ml, loosely packed) finely chopped fresh mint
1½ cups (375 ml) finely chopped fresh flat-leaf parsley
1½ cups (375 ml) finely chopped rocket
1½ cups (375 ml) crumbled feta cheese
½ cup (125 ml) dried pomegranate seeds or 1 cup (250 ml) fresh ones (see Notes)
1 large head of broccoli
¾ cup (180 ml) walnuts, coarsely chopped
1½ cups (375 ml) Vinaigrette (p. 186), made with 300 ml oil and 45 ml each lemon juice and white wine vinegar
2 cloves garlic, peeled and crushed
1 Tbsp (15 ml) sumac (see Notes) or 2 tsp (10 ml) finely grated lemon zest
salt and milled black pepper
extra feta cheese and walnuts, for topping

Put the rice, salt and cold water into a pot, bring to the boil and cook at a lively simmer for 16–18 minutes, or until the rice is tender. Rinse the rice in a colander under running water for 1 minute to wash off excess starch, then allow to cool to lukewarm in the colander, fluffing the grains now and then with a fork. Transfer the rice into a large mixing bowl and add the herbs, feta and pomegranate seeds. Break the broccoli into florets and, using the coarse teeth of a cheese grater, grate their upper surfaces to a depth of about 3 mm, to create a pile of green 'crumbs'. Add these crumbs and the walnuts to the salad (keep the leftover broccoli for another dish).

Mix the vinaigrette with the garlic and sumac, pour it over the salad and season to taste with salt and pepper. Toss the salad well and allow to stand for at least 30 minutes. Tip onto a platter and scatter lavishly with some extra crumbled feta and broken walnuts.

Serves 8 as a side salad.

Notes

This salad keeps well in the fridge for up to 24 hours, but add the walnuts just before you serve it. If you'd like to serve this as a starter, halve the recipe. Dried pomegranate seeds can be found in delicatessens and health shops; if you can't find them, use chopped dried cranberries. Sumac is a tart, lemony Middle Eastern spice, available from good spice shops.

Griddled Courgettes with Mint and Mozzarella

Delicately flavoured as they are, courgettes tend to be overlooked as a salad ingredient. But when griddled to a toasty gold and combined with excellent mozzarella, a lemony dressing and both fresh and dried mint, these Cinderellas of the vegetable world truly get a chance to shine.

16 large, unblemished courgettes
a little olive oil, for frying
juice of 2 lemons
1½ tsp (7.5 ml) hot English mustard powder
1 clove garlic, peeled and very finely grated
2 tsp (10 ml) dried mint
⅔ cup (160 ml) extra-virgin olive oil
salt and milled black pepper
300 g fresh white mozzarella cheese
or bocconcini (see Notes)
½ cup (125 ml) small fresh mint leaves

Cut each courgette lengthways, right through the stalk, into slices about 4 mm thick. Heat a ridged griddle pan for 3–4 minutes, until blazing hot. Rub a film of oil over each courgette slice and cook, in batches, for 2 or 3 minutes on each side, or until just tender and handsomely marked with tiger stripes. If you don't have a griddle pan, fry the slices in a pan with a little olive oil until toasty. Put the warm slices in a big mixing bowl. Combine the lemon juice, mustard powder, garlic and dried mint in a small bowl, whisk in the olive oil and season to taste with salt and pepper.

Pull the mozzarella into large flakes, add it to the courgettes, pour over the dressing and toss gently to coat. Arrange the salad on a platter and scatter with mint leaves. Allow to stand for 30 minutes. Serve at room temperature, with bread.

Serves 8 as a starter or side salad.

Notes | This salad can be made several hours in advance, but keep at room temperature. Add the mint leaves just before you serve it. If you can't find an authentic fresh mozzarella cheese or bocconcini (small mozzarella balls), use good feta instead.

Peppery Tomatoes with Hot Sesame Oil

This dish of sliced ripe tomatoes and fresh herbs (photo, p. 24) is simplicity itself, but its flavours are sensational. Poured with a dramatic sizzle over the salad, the nutty, smoking-hot sesame oil really intensifies the summery flavour and sweetness of the tomatoes.

12 large, ripe tomatoes
4 Tbsp (60 ml) sesame oil
4 tsp (20 ml) Kikkoman soy sauce
2 Tbsp (30 ml) rice wine vinegar or white wine vinegar
4 Tbsp (60 ml) finely chopped fresh flat-leaf parsley
2 Tbsp (30 ml) finely chopped fresh mint
milled black pepper
1 Tbsp (15 ml) sesame seeds

Cut the ends off the tomatoes, slice them thinly and arrange in overlapping circles on a platter. Put the sesame oil in a large soup ladle and heat it directly over a gas flame, until the oil begins to smoke (if you have an electric hob, heat the oil in a frying pan). Pour the blazing-hot oil all over the tomatoes, standing well back as you do so. Drizzle the soy sauce and vinegar over the slices and scatter with parsley and mint. Now add plenty of milled black pepper. You shouldn't need to add any extra salt. Put the sesame seeds in a dry frying pan, toss over a medium heat until lightly toasted and sprinkle them over the salad. Allow to stand for 30 minutes before serving. Serve with crusty bread for mopping up the juices.

Serves 8 as a starter or side salad.

Cauliflower Salad with Crisp-Fried Chorizo

An easy, tapas-style dish with knock-out flavours and textures: shaved raw cauliflower with fried crumbled chorizo, crisp breadcrumbs, a whisper of garlic and a warm lemony olive-oil dressing.

2 small heads of young cauliflower
2 top-quality chorizo sausages, each about 15 cm long
3 Tbsp (45 ml) sunflower or canola oil
3 day-old bread rolls
7 Tbsp (105 ml) extra-virgin olive oil
2 cloves garlic, peeled and finely grated
juice of 2 lemons
½ cup (125 ml) finely chopped fresh flat-leaf parsley
salt and milled black pepper

Break off the cauliflower florets and, using a mandolin or sharp knife, cut them vertically into very thin slices, right through their 'trunks'. Arrange on a platter, putting the most attractive slices on top. Peel the skin off one of the chorizo sausages and crumble the flesh (or cut into a fine dice). Heat the sunflower oil in a pan and fry the sausage bits over a medium heat for a minute or two, or until just crisp. Remove with a slotted spoon and scatter them over the cauliflower. Crumble the bread rolls into the frying pan — you need some pea-sized nuggets, as well as smaller crumbs — and fry until crisp and golden. Drain on kitchen paper.

Discard the oil in the pan and add 1 Tbsp (15 ml) of the olive oil, and the garlic. Gently fry the garlic for a minute or two, then add the lemon juice and stir briskly to dislodge the sediment on the bottom of the pan. Remove from the heat and whisk in the remaining olive oil. Pour the warm dressing over the cauliflower and sprinkle with the breadcrumbs and parsley. Finely slice the remaining sausage and arrange the slices on top of the salad. Grind over plenty of black pepper and season with salt, if necessary. Serve immediately.

Serves 8 as a starter or side salad.

Notes

Prepare an hour or two ahead by slicing the cauliflower and frying the sausage, crumbs (these can be reheated in a moderate oven) and garlic. Leave the garlic in the pan and just before you serve the salad, warm it gently and whisk in the lemon juice and olive oil. Vegetarian option: Use cubes of crisp-fried halloumi cheese (p. 59) in place of chorizo.

Lemony Green Beans with Frizzled Parma Ham and Aïoli

Slim, tender-crisp green beans topped with shards of crisp Parma ham, toasted almonds and a garlicky homemade aïoli.

---

650 g slender green beans, topped and tailed
5 Tbsp (75 ml) extra-virgin olive oil
juice of 1 large lemon
salt and milled black pepper
12 paper-thin slices Parma ham
2 Tbsp (30 ml) sunflower oil, for frying
½ cup (125 ml) flaked almonds

FOR THE AÏOLI
300 ml Mayonnaise (p. 186), made using only olive oil
3 cloves garlic, peeled and crushed (or more, to taste)

Fill a large bowl with cold water and add a handful of ice cubes. Cook the beans in a pot of rapidly boiling salted water for 3–4 minutes, or until the beans are just tender but retain a slight bite. Drain the beans, plunge them into the iced water and leave to chill for 4 minutes. Pat the beans dry, place in a mixing bowl, add the olive oil and lemon juice and toss well to coat. Season to taste with salt and pepper.

To make the aïoli, mix the mayonnaise with the crushed garlic, decant into two small bowls and chill.

Fry the Parma ham slices, a few at a time, in very hot sunflower oil for a minute or so, or until frizzled and crisp. Drain on kitchen paper. Wipe out the pan to remove the oil and toast the flaked almonds over a medium heat for a minute or two, or until golden brown. To serve, pile the beans onto a platter and top with the Parma ham and almonds. Pass the aïoli around in separate bowls.

Serves 8 as a starter or side salad.

Notes | Make the aïoli and toast the almonds up to 36 hours in advance. Green beans turn a muddy khaki if they're left to stand for too long, so put them on to boil no more than 30 minutes before you serve them.

Caesar Salad with Poached Crayfish

Fresh crayfish is so eye-poppingly expensive that I wouldn't dream of serving it as a main course, but I occasionally splash out on a few still-flapping tails, which I craftily stretch across many servings in this, one of the world's best salads. This is an excellent starter for a special occasion but – trust me on this – don't tell anyone that the dressing has anchovies in it.

3 large crayfish tails, in their shells (see Notes)
4 day-old bread rolls
a little olive oil or olive-oil cooking spray
1 x 250 g wedge Parmesan or
Grana Padano
6 baby gem or cos lettuces, about 600 g, or
enough for 8 people

FOR THE DRESSING
2 egg yolks, from extra-large free-range eggs
2 cloves garlic, peeled and sliced
juice of 2 small lemons
2 anchovy fillets, chopped
150 ml extra-virgin olive oil
150 ml sunflower oil
1 Tbsp (15 ml) Worcestershire sauce
salt and milled black pepper

First make the dressing. Put the yolks, garlic, lemon juice and anchovy fillets into the goblet of a blender and whizz until creamy. Now, with the blades turning, trickle the oils onto the egg mixture to form a thick, smooth emulsion. Decant into a small bowl, stir in the Worcestershire sauce and season to taste with salt and pepper. If the sauce seems too thick, thin it by whisking in a few teaspoons of warm water.

Poach the crayfish tails in a large pot of salted, simmering water for 7–8 minutes, or until just cooked through. Drain in a colander for 5 minutes, then pull the flesh from the tails, tear it into flakes (or cut it into cubes), cover and reserve.

Now make the croutons. Heat the oven to 190 °C and place a baking sheet in it to heat. Tear the rolls into large shreds and tatters and brush lightly with olive oil (or spray with olive oil from a can). Place the shredded bread on the heated baking sheet and bake for 5–8 minutes, or until golden and crunchy. Reserve. Finely grate half of the Parmesan.

Assemble the salad at the last moment. Put the lettuce leaves, grated Parmesan and crayfish pieces into a big mixing bowl. Pour over just enough dressing to coat the leaves and very gently toss everything together. Tip the salad onto a large platter, scatter over the croutons and, using a potato peeler, shave generous flakes of the remaining Parmesan all over the salad. Season with salt and pepper and serve immediately.

Serves 8 as a starter or side salad.

Notes

The Caesar dressing improves on standing, so make it the day before. The crayfish can be poached a few hours ahead. Use West Coast rock lobster, as this species is green-listed on the the SASSI database (p. 89).

Beef Fillet and Potato Salad with Green Goddess Dressing

Hot, crisp nuggets of potato take the place of croutons in this substantial, crowd-pleasing salad of leafy greens and rosy fillet slices. The dressing is based on an American recipe of the 1920s, and it looks and tastes as alluring as its name. You can omit the anchovy if you like, but don't leave out the tarragon, which adds a subtle but essential anise note.

1 whole fillet of beef, as big as your budget allows
a little olive oil for rubbing and searing
1 Tbsp (15 ml) cracked black pepper
8 large potatoes, peeled and cut into large cubes
500 g (or enough for 8 people) mixed rocket, watercress and baby spinach
sunflower oil, for roasting
juice of 1 large lemon
8 Tbsp (120 ml) extra-virgin olive oil
100 g Parmesan or Grana Padano

FOR THE DRESSING
1 cup (250 ml) Mayonnaise (p. 186) or Hellmann's original
½ cup (125 ml) cultured buttermilk
4 Tbsp (60 ml) freshly squeezed lemon juice
1 anchovy fillet (optional)
1½ tsp (7.5 ml) Dijon mustard
2 tsp (10 ml) dried tarragon
1 small clove garlic, peeled and sliced
1 large spring onion, white and pale green parts only
3 Tbsp (45 ml) chopped fresh flat-leaf parsley
3 Tbsp (45 ml) finely snipped fresh chives
salt and milled black pepper

Heat the oven to 200 °C.

First make the dressing. Put all the ingredients, except the chives and seasoning, into a blender and whizz until smooth and creamy. Don't over-blend the dressing: it should be lightly flecked with green. Stir in the chives and season to taste with salt and pepper. Chill.

Pat the fillet dry, rub with a little olive oil and roll in the cracked black pepper. Heat some oil in a large pan until blazing hot and sear the fillet on all sides for 4–5 minutes to create a dark, caramelised crust. Place on a baking sheet and roast for 15–25 minutes, or until done to your liking (see Notes). Rest on a plate for 10 minutes, then cover and refrigerate.

Cook the potatoes in boiling salted water for 7 minutes, or until their outer surfaces are just soft. Drain the potatoes in a colander, then vigorously toss them to roughen their surfaces. Chill, uncovered, until you need them.

Forty-five minutes before you're ready to serve the salad, toss the potato cubes in a little sunflower oil and roast at 190 °C for 40–50 minutes, or until crunchy and golden. When the potatoes are almost done, arrange the salad leaves in a large bowl and dress with the lemon juice and olive oil. Season with salt and pepper. Cut the fillet into thin slices and arrange them on top of the leaves. Shave the Parmesan, using a potato peeler, all over the salad, scatter over the hot roast potatoes and take immediately to the table. Pass the dressing around in a separate jug.

Serves 8 as a main course.

Notes

How long you roast the fillet for will depend on its size and your oven. A large fillet takes about 20 minutes after the initial browning to cook to a light, rosy pink on the inside; a slim fillet will take 12–15 minutes. If you're unsure, cut a small slit in the underside of the fillet to check for doneness.

New-Potato Salad with Avocado, Wasabi and Seared Tuna

My light, bright twist on everyone's favourite salad: tender baby potatoes combined with mayonnaise, creamy avocado and nose-zapping wasabi paste, then topped with a shower of snipped chives and strips of seared tuna.

1.5 kg new potatoes
1 Tbsp (15 ml) salt
4 ripe Hass or Fuerte avocados
3 Tbsp (45 ml) olive or sunflower oil
4 large fresh tuna steaks, weighing about 600 g
⅓ cup (80 ml) finely snipped fresh chives

FOR THE DRESSING
½ onion, peeled and very finely chopped or grated
juice of 2 small lemons
1½ tsp (7.5 ml) white sugar
1 cup (250 ml) Mayonnaise (p. 186) or Hellmann's original
1 cup (250 ml) thick natural yoghurt
1 large clove garlic, peeled and crushed
3–4 tsp (15–20 ml) wasabi paste, or more, to taste
1 tsp (5 ml) Tabasco sauce
salt and milled black pepper

Cook the potatoes in plenty of rapidly boiling salted water for 10–15 minutes, or until quite tender when pierced with the tip of a sharp knife, but not splitting or falling apart. Drain in a colander, then cut each potato in half (leave the smallest ones whole).

To make the dressing, combine the onion, lemon juice and sugar in a large mixing bowl and set aside for 5 minutes (the lemon juice will take the sting out of the onions). Whisk in the mayonnaise, yoghurt, garlic, wasabi and Tabasco and season to taste with salt and pepper.

Peel the avocados, cut them into large cubes and immediately add them to the dressing. Tip in the warm cooked potatoes and toss very gently to combine.

Heat the oil in a large frying pan and, when it's blazing hot but not smoking, fry the tuna steaks, in batches, for 2–3 minutes on each side, or until nice and toasty on the outside but still rosy pink inside. Season with salt, pepper and a spritz of lemon juice.

Tip the potato salad into a large serving bowl and scatter over the chives. Slice the tuna and arrange the slices over the salad. Serve at room temperature.

Serves 8 as a main course.

Notes

You can make the potato salad in advance, but add the avocado cubes, and sear the tuna, just before you serve it.

Soups

A bowl of fragrant soup has Home and Mum written all over it, and that is why it's such a good way to begin a wonderful feast on a frosty winter night (or a scorching summer's day, for that matter). With three provisos ...

First, it needs to be a really good soup, with some element of drama or surprise: a vibrant, eye-socking colour, or flavours so intense and surprising they tie your tongue in happy knots, or an ethereal taste and delicate texture. A humdrum butternut soup, a watery minestrone or a lentil sludge will just not do for a proper feast, and you can expect glum faces around the table if your soup doesn't deliver a high-kicking cabaret in a bowl.

Second, your soup needs to be dished out, if it is a starter course, in restrained servings. I've often been presented with a bowl brimming with what seems like an ocean of scalding (or, worse, lukewarm) gloop, and my heart always sinks because I know I have to gulp down the lot or risk offending the cook. No soup should be eaten out of duty.

I suggest you put a tureen of soup in the middle of the table and ask guests to help themselves. If the soup needs to be plated individually, allow 1 cup (250 ml) of soup per person; this is more than enough for a starter portion. If you're serving the soup as the main course, allow 350–450 ml per person. If it's an iced soup, allow 125–200 ml each.

Third, there is no point in making most of the soups in this chapter unless you use a good homemade stock. I try not to be a food snob, but I have never come across a powder or cube that is a patch on proper homemade stock. Packaged stocks taste dusty, are overly salty and — most important — they don't have the depth and complexity needed to produce soups with singing flavours. If you aren't already in the habit of making your own stocks (p. 187), I urge you to give them a go. Stocks are easy and economical to make and they freeze beautifully.

Because soups usually call for humble ingredients, this is one part of a feast where I feel I can splash out on rare and expensive toppings — white-truffle oil, for instance, or a few slices of excellent smoked salmon or trout. And toppings are important: most children under eight, for example, will slope off into the garden when they see soup arrive at the table, but quickly change their minds when they realise they can customise their soups with grated cheese *and* crispy bacon *and* croutons *and* cream.

White Gazpacho with Tomato Granita

An iced soup that will bring you rapturous applause on the hottest days of summer. This is spectacular served in pretty bowls made of ice because the bottom of the soup partially freezes, creating a surprise layer of zingy ice cream. This isn't an authentic gazpacho because it contains yoghurt, but with its topping of feathery flakes of iced fresh tomato juice, it certainly tastes like one. Even better, I think.

2 extra-large free-range egg yolks
1 clove garlic, peeled and sliced
2 thin slices fresh white bread, crusts cut off
2 Tbsp (30 ml) white wine vinegar
5 Tbsp (75 ml) extra-virgin olive oil
2 English cucumbers, peeled and cubed
6 slim spring onions, white and pale green parts only, sliced
1 small green pepper, chopped
4 large sprigs pale celery leaves, taken from the heart of the bunch
4 Tbsp (60 ml) chopped fresh flat-leaf parsley
2 cups (500 ml) thick natural yoghurt
2 cups (500 ml) iced water
salt and milled black pepper

FOR THE TOMATO GRANITA
400 g ripe cherry tomatoes
1 tsp (5 ml) lemon juice
2 tsp (10 ml) Tabasco sauce
salt and milled black pepper

First make the granita. Place a shallow metal dish (a cake pan is ideal) in the freezer for 1 hour. Purée the cherry tomatoes in a blender and tip the mixture into a sieve set over a bowl. Press down on the puréed tomatoes with the back of a soup ladle to extract all the juice. Discard the pulp, stir in the lemon juice and Tabasco and season with salt and pepper. Pour into the cold dish and freeze for 30–45 minutes, or until the mixture is set at the edges. Using a fork, scrape and scratch the frozen edges to create crystalline flakes. Freeze for another 20–30 minutes (set a timer to remind yourself), scrape again, and continue freezing and scraping, working inwards to the middle of the dish, until you have a fluffy pile of coral-pink ice flakes. Keep covered in the freezer until the last minute.

Put the yolks, garlic, bread, vinegar and 2 Tbsp (30 ml) of the oil into a blender and whizz to a paste. Add the remaining olive oil in a steady stream and blend to a thick emulsion. Add the remaining soup ingredients – in batches, if necessary – and process until smooth and creamy. Pour the soup into a large non-metallic bowl, cover and chill for at least 3 hours. Ladle the cold soup into chilled bowls, add a few ice cubes and a pyramid of granita, and take immediately to the table. If you're serving this in homemade ice bowls (see Notes), there's no need to add the ice cubes.

Serves 8.

Notes

The flavour of this soup improves after a few hours of chilling, but it should be served on the day it is made. The granita can be made a day or two in advance. Make the ice bowls in batches, starting up to 3 days ahead. Arrange four 1-cm-thick slices of cherry tomato in the bottom of a plastic or ceramic soup bowl. Balance another, smaller bowl on top (there should be a gap of at least 1 cm between the bowls). Wedge a few more tomato slices into the gap so it's even all round, and tuck in some fresh coriander sprigs and small red chillies. Fill the gap with cold water and freeze for 4 hours, or until solid. To unmould, dip the bottom bowl into hot water, and run some more hot water into the top bowl. Wrap each bowl in clingfilm and keep in the freezer until needed. To serve, place each bowl on a small plate and tuck a napkin or thick paper serviette under each one to stop it from sliding around.

Onion Soup with a Mustard and Cheese Soufflé Topping

I think French onion soup is one of the world's greatest dishes: easy and inexpensive, yet so comforting, delicious and sustaining. Take your time cooking the onions, because this is the key to a deep and complex flavour. This dish is inspired by a recipe in Robert Carrier's 1963 book *Great Dishes of the World*, a trusty reference that has been at my elbow for two decades.

1.3 kg (about 9) onions, peeled
100 g (100 ml) butter
2 cloves garlic, peeled and finely chopped
4 tsp (20 ml) balsamic vinegar
1 bay leaf
2 large sprigs fresh thyme
1 tsp (5 ml) salt
1 Tbsp (15 ml) cake flour
2.4 litres vegetable or chicken stock
salt and milled black pepper

FOR THE SOUFFLÉ TOPPING
6 Tbsp (90 ml/90 g) butter
5 Tbsp (75 ml) cake flour
600 ml milk
2 cups (500 ml, loosely packed) grated Cheddar or Gruyère
2 Tbsp (30 ml) wholegrain mustard
6 extra-large free-range eggs, separated
salt and milled black pepper
5 Tbsp (75 ml) grated Parmesan

Thinly slice the onions. Melt the butter in a large, heavy-based pot and add the onions, garlic, vinegar, bay leaf, thyme and salt. Cook over a very low heat, stirring occasionally, for 1 ¼ hours, or until the onions have reduced to a sticky, deep-golden tangle. Turn up the heat a bit, stir in the flour and cook, stirring, for 1 minute. Pour in the stock, stir well and bring to the boil. Turn down the heat again and bubble gently, uncovered, for 30 minutes. Remove the bay leaf and thyme sprigs and season the soup with plenty of salt and pepper.

Heat the oven to 180 °C.

To make the soufflé topping, first make a béchamel sauce (p. 188) with the butter, flour and milk. Take the pan off the heat, add the grated cheese and mustard and stir until the cheese has melted and the sauce is smooth. Allow to cool for a few minutes, stirring now and then to prevent a skin forming.

Lightly whisk the egg yolks and mix them into the sauce. Season to taste with salt and pepper. Whisk the egg whites with a pinch of salt until stiff (but not dry), and then mix a ladleful into the sauce to slacken it. Now, very gently, fold in the remaining whites.

Grease the inside rims of eight soup bowls so the soufflé can glide easily upwards. Place the bowls on two large, sturdy baking sheets and divide the warm soup among them. Gently spoon large dollops of the soufflé mixture on top of the soup, coaxing it right to the edges of the bowls so the soup is completely covered. Sprinkle a little grated Parmesan on top and bake at 180 °C for 15–20 minutes, or until the soufflés are puffed and golden but still slightly wobbly in the middle.

Serves 8.

Notes

Make the onion soup up to 2 days in advance. The whites must be folded into the soufflé mix immediately before it's baked, but you can make the béchamel sauce up to 8 hours ahead. If you're expecting a crowd and doubling the recipe, make this in a large ovenproof pot, pile all the soufflé mix on top and increase the cooking time by about 10 minutes.

Spring Onion and Celery Soup with Smoked Trout

With its beautiful pale jade colour and subtle flavours, this soup is good on its own, but delightful topped with flakes of lightly smoked Franschhoek trout (photo, p. 40). Added cold, the trout half-poaches in the soup's residual heat, contributing an intriguing smoky note. Straining this soup is laborious but well worth the effort to achieve a fine, smooth result.

30 slim spring onions (about 3 bunches)
6 x 20-cm stalks young celery, taken from the heart of the bunch
4 Tbsp (60 ml/60 g) butter
1 clove garlic, peeled and finely chopped
1.75 litres vegetable or chicken stock
1 cup (250 ml) milk
3 medium potatoes, peeled and finely sliced
2 tsp (10 ml) cornflour
200 ml fresh cream
salt and white pepper
10 slices lightly smoked Franschhoek trout or smoked salmon
olive oil
small sprigs of fresh dill

Trim the roots and dark green tops of the spring onions (you'll use only the white and pale green parts) and slice. Trim and slice the celery stalks. Chop the pale green leaves and set them to one side. Melt the butter in a soup pot, add the spring onions, sliced celery stalks and garlic and cover their surface with a circle of baking paper, or the wrapper from a block of butter. Cook over a low heat for 12–15 minutes, or until very soft. Remove the paper, add the stock, milk, potatoes and reserved celery leaves and bring to the boil. Turn down the heat and simmer for 25 minutes, skimming off any foam as it rises.

Blend the soup to a smooth purée and strain it through a fine sieve into the rinsed-out pot. Mix the cornflour and 2 Tbsp (30 ml) of the cream to a smooth paste and add this to the soup, stirring constantly as it comes to the boil. Simmer for 3 minutes, then stir in the remaining cream. Season to taste with salt and white pepper.

Cut the smoked trout into pieces no bigger than the bowl of a soup spoon. Ladle the hot soup into bowls, swirl with a little olive oil and a drizzle of cream, and top each with tiny sprigs of dill and a few pieces of trout. Serve immediately.

Serves 8.

Notes

Make this up to 24 hours ahead, then heat and add the trout and dill at the last moment. This is a thinnish soup, but it should not be watery. Add a little more cornflour paste if the consistency seems too thin.

Roasted Ratatouille Soup with Basil Mayonnaise

A beautiful mingling of jewel-bright Mediterranean vegetables roasted in the oven, whizzed to a brick-red purée and topped with a flurry of basil mayonnaise. The taste of this summery soup depends a lot on the quality of the vegetables: choose plump, sleek, unblemished specimens at the peak of their ripeness.

8 large ripe, juicy tomatoes
2 large, plump aubergines
3 red peppers
12 courgettes
3 onions, peeled
4 sprigs of fresh thyme
150 ml olive oil
flaky sea salt and milled black pepper
6 large cloves garlic
2 litres vegetable or chicken stock

FOR THE BASIL MAYONNAISE
1 cup (250 ml, loosely packed) fresh basil leaves
salt
300 ml Mayonnaise (p. 186), made with lemon juice, not vinegar
milled black pepper

Heat the oven to 200 °C.

Top and tail the tomatoes, aubergines, peppers, courgettes and onions and cut into slices about 1 cm thick. Place the vegetables and thyme sprigs in a deep roasting pan. Drizzle with the olive oil, season with salt and pepper and toss so each slice is coated. Tuck the unpeeled garlic cloves deep into a corner of the vegetable bed (but take note of where you've hidden them). Roast for 30 minutes, or until the vegetables are golden brown in patches. Cover the pan with foil, reduce the heat to 180 °C and bake for a further 30 minutes, or until the vegetables are tender. Retrieve the garlic cloves and snip off the pointy ends. Squeeze the warm pulp onto a plate, cover with clingfilm and reserve. Pour the stock into the pan, cover again with foil and bake at the same temperature for another 15 minutes.

Using a mortar and pestle, pound the basil leaves, a pinch of salt and a third of the reserved cooked garlic pulp to a paste. Stir this into the mayonnaise, season with pepper, and add more salt and lemon juice if necessary. Cover and chill.

Tip the contents of the roasting pan into a soup pot, discard the thyme sprigs, add the remaining garlic pulp and whizz to a thick purée using a stick blender. (Or blitz the soup, in batches, in a blender.) If the soup seems too thick, thin it down with hot water. Season to taste with salt and pepper. Serve piping hot, topped with a dollop of cold basil mayonnaise.

Serves 8.

Notes

Although this soup can be made well in advance, it's best served on the same day you make it. Make the mayonnaise up to two days ahead, but prepare and add the basil paste no more than 2 hours ahead, or the basil may blacken.

Spicy Gem Squash Mini-Tureens

Gem squash is a vegetable dear to the hearts of South Africans, but it's almost always served one way: halved, boiled and dobbled with butter. Here's an entirely new way to eat gems: turn them into dear little tureens, fill them with a fragrant, lightly curried coconut sauce and slow-bake them to a melting tenderness. Choose large, hard-skinned gems: much of the pleasure in eating this soup comes from scooping out the spaghetti-like strands found mostly in squashes of a certain age.

8 mature gem squashes, each the size of a grapefruit
4 Tbsp (60 ml) sunflower oil
1 stick of cinnamon
3 cardamom pods, cracked
10 small dried curry leaves
1½ tsp (7.5 ml) black mustard seeds
2 large onions, peeled and very finely chopped
a thumb-size piece of fresh ginger, finely grated
3 cloves garlic, peeled and finely chopped
1 tsp (5 ml) salt
600 ml coconut milk
2 tsp (10 ml) ground cumin
1 tsp (5 ml) chilli powder
1 tsp (5 ml) ground coriander
1 tsp (5 ml) turmeric
1½ cups (375 ml) water
2 Tbsp (30 ml) lemon juice, plus a little extra
milled black pepper

Heat the oven to 180 °C.

Carefully cut a small lid off the stalk end of each squash (this is tricky; see Notes for tips), scoop out the seeds and reserve the lids. Heat the oil in a large pan and add the cinnamon, cardamom pods, curry leaves and mustard seeds. Fry over a high heat until the mustard seeds begin to sputter and pop. Add the onions, ginger, garlic and salt and cook, over a medium heat, for 6–7 minutes, or until the onions are golden and sticky. Don't allow the garlic to scorch. Add the coconut milk and remaining spices and bubble over a low heat for 10 minutes, or until slightly thickened. Stir in the water and lemon juice and cook for another 3 minutes. Season to taste. Discard the cinnamon and cardamom.

Place each squash on a square of heavy foil large enough to enclose the squash completely. Fill each to within 1 cm of its rim (you should have some liquid left over in the pan after filling the squashes; reserve this) and press its lid into place. Close the foil parcels tightly, place in a roasting pan and bake for 1 hour. Remove the pan from the oven and unwrap the top of each parcel, leaving the squashes sitting on cupped nests of foil. Remove the lids and top up each tureen with a little of the reserved sauce plus a spritz of lemon juice. Replace the lids (but don't close the foil) and return to the oven. Reduce the heat to 150 °C and bake for another hour, or until the flesh inside is very tender. Serve piping hot with sliced, warmed naan bread or some crisp poppadums for dipping.

Serves 8.

Notes

Make the sauce and fill the squashes up to 24 hours ahead. The easiest way to remove the tops of the gems is to score the skin firmly all round with a sturdy craft knife. Now insert the blade of a heavy knife into the cut and firmly smack the back of the blade, turning the squash as you go. Don't worry if the lids look ragged or uneven: they will shrink into perky little bonnets during cooking. Choose hard squashes that will not collapse or topple over in the oven. I always look for ones with pretty yellow speckles and stripes.

Thai-Spiced Tomato and Seafood Soup

This soul-warming broth is one of my happy-hybrid recipes, featuring both the tingling aromatics of Southeast Asia and the deep, lip-smacking flavour of tomato-based Mediterranean fish soups. Very fresh, firm white linefish is essential, but you can get away with frozen tubes of tender Patagonian calamari and frozen mussels on the half-shell.

FOR THE PASTE
10 small dried red chillies
2 x 20-cm stalks fresh lemongrass
½ onion, peeled and chopped
4 cloves garlic, peeled and chopped
a thumb-size piece of fresh ginger, grated
4 fresh lime leaves or 6 dried ones, chopped
3 Tbsp (45 ml) chopped fresh coriander roots (see Notes)
1 tsp (5 ml) chilli powder
1 tsp (5 ml) ground cumin
1 tsp (5ml) ground coriander
½ tsp (2.5 ml) turmeric
1 Tbsp (15 ml) sunflower oil

FOR THE SOUP
2 Tbsp (30 ml) sunflower oil
600 ml coconut milk
1½ cups (375 ml) tomato juice (the sort you'd use to make a cocktail)
2 Tbsp (30 ml) tomato paste
4 cups (1 litre) hot water or fish stock
2 tsp (10 ml) paprika
6 fresh lime leaves or 8 dried ones, or 1 Tbsp (15 ml) finely grated lime zest
5 tsp (25 ml) fish sauce, or more, to taste
salt and milled black pepper
600 g fresh white linefish, skinned, boned and cut into large cubes
24 mussels, cleaned
12 small calamari tubes, cleaned and sliced
2–3 Tbsp (30–45 ml) lime juice, fresh if possible
a small bunch of fresh coriander, leaves picked

First make the paste. Cover the chillies with boiling water, weigh them down so they're submerged and soak for 15 minutes. Bruise the lemongrass with a rolling pin, peel away the tough outer layer and finely slice. Drain the chillies and put them, the lemongrass and the remaining paste ingredients into a blender, and process to a paste. If the blades are reluctant to turn, add a little more oil.

To make the soup, heat the sunflower oil in a large pot, add 4 Tbsp (60 ml) of the paste and fry over a medium heat for a minute or two. Add the coconut milk, tomato juice, tomato paste, hot water, paprika, lime leaves (or zest) and fish sauce, season with salt and pepper and cook at a brisk simmer for 15 minutes. Add another tablespoon of the spice paste (or more, to taste) and cook for a further 5 minutes.

Immediately before you serve the soup, add the seafood. Put the fish in first and simmer very gently for 4–6 minutes, or until the fish is just cooked through. Now add the mussels and calamari and simmer for another 2–3 minutes. If you're using fresh mussels, discard any that don't open in the soup. Stir in the lime juice. Taste the soup to make sure it has a good balance of sweet and sour, hot and salty, and add more lime juice and fish sauce, if required. Scatter with coriander leaves and serve immediately.

Notes

Make the soup up to 6 hours ahead, but add the seafood immediately before you serve it. Don't boil the soup vigorously, or the texture of the seafood will be ruined. Prawns may be used in place of calamari.

Look in Asian stores for bunches of coriander with roots still attached. If you can't find coriander root, use the stalks of the coriander.

A stick blender with a small jug-and-blade attachment is best for making the paste, but you can make it in a powerful blender. Or pound it to a paste using a mortar and pestle.

Vegetables, Pulses and Pasta

Vegetarians are always delighted when you provide interesting non-meaty dishes at a feast, but their pleasure quickly turns to alarm, then indignation, when the other guests at the table fall like starving orphans on 'their' food.

I appreciate how annoying it must be to see the vegetarian options being gobbled in a flash, but the truth is that meat-eaters are also omnivores and (speaking as one) they are just as keen on substantial vegetable and cheese dishes as any vegetarian. My advice is to assume that everyone will eat the non-meaty dishes with equal gusto and to make more than enough to go around. I've been to many a wedding where the cheese-and-vegetable 'alternative' has vanished within minutes of the buffet queue opening, leaving red — and hungry — faces all round.

While writing this chapter, I canvassed all the vegetarians and vegans I know — and many I don't know, via the Internet — to find out what special dish they'd be thankful for at a feast. Lasagnes, roulades, stuffed vegetables, falafels, cleverly spiced curries and crunchy salads came out tops, with aubergines, mushrooms, tofu and all sorts of cheeses being the top-ranking ingredients. Interestingly, the overwhelming sentiment was a plea for variety. 'Vegetarians are often offered a stodgy dish slathered in white sauce, or a bland stuffed butternut, and they're expected to make do with this and some green salad,' commented one person. 'But what I really appreciate is being able to help myself to a plateful of three or four different dishes with a variety of appealing tastes and textures.'

In this chapter I've included a selection of vegetable dishes, some designed to satisfy the cravings of neglected vegetarians, others more simple vegetable accompaniments that everyone will enjoy. And, on the subject of vegetables: the key to choosing knock-out side dishes is to select excellent ingredients that are in high season (with the exception of potatoes, carrots and top-quality frozen peas, which are good at any time of the year). I always visit one or two good supermarkets the day before a feast to pick out sleek, snappy, fat-cheeked specimens of the best local produce, and then I build dishes around them.

This chapter also contains some substantial dishes using pasta and pulses, and some that contain meaty elements. If there are vegetarians on your guest list, set aside a portion of these dishes before you add the chicken or meat.

Asparagus with Egg Mimosa, Butter and Breadcrumbs

Based on a classic 'Polonaise' dressing, this topping may be old fashioned, but it's a time-tested classic for a reason: beautifully crunchy, indulgently buttery and so pretty strewn over fresh asparagus. Cooked, sieved egg yolks are called 'mimosa' because they resemble the fluffy yellow flowers of the plant of the same name.

3 extra-large free-range eggs
2 slices white bread, a day or two old
48 spears fresh asparagus
1 cup (250 ml/250 g) butter
a big pinch of white pepper
⅓ cup (80 ml) finely chopped fresh parsley
salt
juice of 1 lemon

Hard boil the eggs in briskly simmering water for 9 minutes, then plunge into cold water. Set under a trickling tap for 3 minutes, or until completely cooled. Peel the eggs, remove the yolks and, using the back of a spoon, press the yolks through a metal sieve. Cover with clingfilm and reserve. Finely chop the whites and keep covered in a separate bowl.

Whizz the bread slices to a medium crumb in a food processor and set aside. Cut the woody bases off the asparagus spears and cook in rapidly boiling salted water for 3–5 minutes – depending on their thickness – or until just tender, but with a slight bite. In the meantime, heat the butter in a large frying pan and add the white pepper. When the butter stops foaming, tip in the breadcrumbs and fry over a medium heat until crunchy and a light golden colour (the crumbs will continue to cook after you remove them from the heat, so whip them off well before they begin to darken). Cool for 1 minute, then stir in the chopped egg whites and parsley. Season with salt to taste.

Drain the asparagus in a colander, pat dry with kitchen paper, pile onto a large warmed platter and squeeze over the lemon juice. Tip the breadcrumb mixture over the spears and toss gently to coat. Scatter with the sieved yolks and serve immediately.

Serves 8 as a starter or side dish.

Notes

The crunchy crumb topping must be made immediately before you serve the dish, but you can chop the parsley and cook and chop the eggs an hour or two in advance (keep them tightly covered in the fridge). If you'd like to serve the asparagus cold, plunge the spears into iced water immediately after you cook them; this will preserve their fresh green colour.

Baby Mielies with Zesty Smoked Butter

Tender spears of baby sweetcorn are good with plain butter and salt, but sensational with smoked butter and some vibrant Mexican flavours. Cook the mielies over hot coals if you have time to fire up the braai, or use a ridged griddle pan to give them some toasty tiger stripes.

48 baby mielies or 8 whole mielies, sliced crossways into thirds

FOR THE BUTTER
½ cup (125 ml/125 g) salted butter, softened
½ cup (125 ml/125 g) smoked butter, softened (see Notes)
2 fresh red chillies, deseeded and finely chopped
finely grated zest of 1 large lemon or 2 small limes
2 Tbsp (30 ml) lemon or lime juice
2 cloves garlic, peeled and finely grated
5 Tbsp (75 ml) finely chopped fresh coriander
salt and milled black pepper

To make the flavoured butter, put all the ingredients in a bowl, whisk until smooth and season to taste with salt and pepper (go easy on the salt, as the butter is already quite salty). Chill the mixture for 20 minutes, or until it's just firm enough to hold its shape. Put a long piece of clingfilm on the counter, spoon the butter into a 15-cm-long strip on top, tightly roll up the plastic and twist the ends to form a neat salami-like shape. Chill until hard, then slice into 7-mm-thick discs and refrigerate, covered, on a plate, until needed. Alternatively, place tablespoonful-sized dollops on a sheet of baking paper and refrigerate until firm.

Braai the mielies over gentle coals until freckled with brown and just tender. Or cook them on a very hot ridged griddle pan, or for 5–6 minutes in plenty of rapidly boiling salted water. Tip onto a large warmed platter and serve piping hot with discs or blobs of cold flavoured butter.

Serves 8 as a side dish or starter.

Notes

If you're making these in advance, toss the hot mielies in 2 Tbsp (30 ml) of the flavoured butter. Cover with clingfilm and refrigerate until needed. Place, covered with foil, in a hot oven for 10 minutes before you serve them. Smoked butter is available from good delicatessens; if you can't find it, use 250 g ordinary butter and add 1½ tsp (7.5 ml) smoked paprika to the mixture.

Braised Baby Leeks with Halloumi 'Popcorn'

The leek may be a humble vegetable, but it is capable of great nobility. The French refer to leeks as *l'asperges du pauvre*, or 'the asparagus of the poor', and it's not difficult to see why. Young, tender leeks gently softened in butter, or braised with white wine and herbs, are delicate and delicious. Slow-braised baby leeks have a lovely melting texture, so they need to be paired with something crunchy. Here, I've used nuggets of crisp-fried halloumi cheese, but the leeks are also good with fried crumbled bacon or pan-frizzled slices of Parma ham.

32 slim baby leeks, or enough for 8 people
5 Tbsp (75 ml/75 g) butter
a large (15 cm) sprig of rosemary
2 cloves garlic, peeled and halved
6 Tbsp (90 ml) dry white wine
2 Tbsp (30 ml) water
salt and milled black pepper
juice of 1 lemon
5 Tbsp (75 ml) extra-virgin olive oil
¾ cup (180 ml) fresh breadcrumbs
sunflower oil for frying
150 g halloumi cheese

Rinse the leeks and trim off the roots and dark green leaves. Heat the butter over a medium heat in a large frying pan and add the whole leeks, rosemary and garlic. Cook, tossing now and then, for 5–7 minutes, or until the leeks begin to turn golden. Don't allow the garlic to scorch. Add the wine and water and season to taste with salt and black pepper. Cover the surface of the leeks with a circle of baking paper (or the wrapper from a block of butter), turn the heat right down and braise gently for 15 minutes, or until the leeks are very tender and the liquid has reduced to a few teaspoons. Remove the paper, turn up the heat, add the lemon juice and olive oil and bubble briskly for 30 seconds. Remove from the heat, cover and set aside.

Just before you serve the leeks, fry the breadcrumbs in 2 Tbsp (30 ml) of sunflower oil until golden and crisp (p. 55). Drain on kitchen paper. Wipe out the pan, pour in enough oil to cover its base to a depth of 3 mm and turn up the heat. Pat the halloumi dry on kitchen paper and cut it into small (about 5-mm) cubes. When the oil is very hot, tilt the pan and fry the halloumi in the 'deep end', in batches. As the cubes puff up and turn golden, remove them with a slotted spoon and drain on kitchen paper. Arrange the leeks on a large platter, or on eight individual plates. Pour over the braising liquid and scatter with the crisp breadcrumbs and halloumi. Serve hot or warm, with bread.

Serves 8 as a side dish or starter.

Notes	Braise the leeks up to 6 hours ahead and gently reheat them before you whisk in the lemon juice and olive oil. The cheese and breadcrumbs should be fried immediately before serving.

Gado-Gado

This delicious and unusual dish of cooked vegetables, crisp salad ingredients and boiled eggs smothered with a piping-hot, spicy peanut sauce is my take on Gado-Gado, a dish popular all over Indonesia. There are many variations of this recipe, so you can happily make it your own by adding any other seasonal vegetables you fancy: mung bean sprouts, radishes, baby mielies, shredded Chinese cabbage, and so on.

24 new potatoes
6 large carrots, peeled and cut into batons
1 small head of cauliflower, broken into florets
500 g slim green beans, topped and tailed
6 extra-large free-range eggs
2 cos lettuces
1 large English cucumber
500 g ripe cherry tomatoes
a packet of shrimp crackers (optional)

FOR THE SAUCE

2 cups (500 ml) roasted, salted peanuts
about 1½ cups (375 ml) hot water
4 cloves garlic, peeled and chopped
3 Tbsp (45 ml) grated fresh ginger
5 spring onions, white parts only, sliced
1 stalk lemongrass, finely sliced
2 small dried chillies, chopped (or more, to taste)
3 Tbsp (45 ml) sunflower or olive oil
1 x 400 ml tin coconut milk
½ tsp (2.5 ml) turmeric
1 tsp (5 ml) salt
2 tsp (10 ml) fish sauce (optional)
2 Tbsp (30 ml) grated palm sugar or 1 Tbsp (15 ml) brown sugar
2 Tbsp (30 ml) Kikkoman soy sauce
2 Tbsp (30 ml) lime juice, fresh or bottled

For the sauce, rinse the peanuts under running water for 30 seconds to remove excess salt. Using a mini blender, grind the peanuts to a wet, slightly chunky paste, adding just enough hot water (about 1½ cups) to help the blades turn freely. Tip the peanut paste into a bowl, leaving 3 Tbsp (45 ml) behind in the blender. Put the garlic, ginger, spring onions, lemongrass and chillies into the blender and process to a fairly fine paste, adding a little oil if necessary.

Fry this spice paste in oil over a medium heat for 2 minutes. Stir in the reserved peanut paste and all the remaining sauce ingredients, turn down the heat and simmer gently for 10 minutes. If the sauce bubbles volcanically, whisk in a little hot water to thin it. Season to taste and add a little more lime juice if you think it needs it.

Cook the vegetables, one type at a time, in plenty of briskly boiling salted water until just tender, but nowhere near mushy. New potatoes take 12–16 minutes, carrot batons 7 minutes, cauliflower florets 5 minutes and green beans 4 minutes. Refresh the carrots, cauliflower and beans under cold running water as they come out of the pot. Pat the vegetables dry, arrange in groups on a tray and cover with clingfilm until needed. Hard boil the eggs in briskly simmering water for 9 minutes and cool completely under a running tap.

Arrange the lettuce leaves on a large platter. Halve the cucumber lengthways, scrape out the seeds and cut into crescents. Cut the tomatoes in half crossways. Peel the eggs and cut each one lengthways into six wedges. Arrange the cooked and raw vegetables, in groups, on top of the lettuce, and tuck in the egg wedges. Heat the peanut sauce and drizzle it, piping hot, over the vegetables (or pass it round in a jug). Top with a scattering of shrimp crackers if desired.

Serves 8.

Notes

This is delicious when the vegetables are warm. Prepare them all in advance as described above, then quickly reheat them in a very hot oven, on a baking sheet covered with foil, for 5–6 minutes before arranging them on top of the salad ingredients. If you don't have a powerful blender, use 1 cup (250 ml) of chunky peanut butter instead of whole salted peanuts.

Spiced Buttered Carrots

This may seem like a lot of carrots for eight people, but this easy dish is so delicious, buttery and comforting that there never seems to be enough to go around. This is my lightly spiced version of the classic French dish Carrots Vichy, with citrus and ginger adding fragrance, and poppy seeds a slight crunch. The important thing here is perfectly cooked carrots: neither *al dente* nor mushy, but at a point somewhere in between.

2 kg carrots
8 Tbsp (120 ml/120 g) butter
3 Tbsp (45 ml) finely grated fresh ginger
a large strip of fresh lime or lemon peel,
white pith removed
1 stick of cinnamon
4 tsp (20 ml) honey
salt and milled black pepper
1½ tsp (7.5 ml) ground cumin
2 tsp (10 ml) ground coriander
1 tsp (5 ml) red chilli powder
2 tsp (10 ml) poppy seeds
fresh lime or lemon juice

Top, tail and peel the carrots and cut them into thick, neat batons about the size of your little finger. Place in a large, shallow pan (an electric frying pan is ideal) and add just enough water to barely cover them (a few ends and edges should poke up out of the water). Add the butter, ginger, citrus peel, cinnamon stick, honey and ½ tsp (2.5 ml) of salt. Turn the heat up to medium-high and cook the carrots at a brisk bubble for 10 minutes, or until they are just tender and the liquid in the pan has reduced to a few tablespoons of syrupy glaze. Turn down the heat and stir in the cumin, coriander, chilli powder and poppy seeds. Cook, gently tossing the mixture now and then, for another 2 minutes, or until the carrots are coated in a rich buttery varnish. Don't allow the spices to brown or burn. Now add a generous spritz of lime or lemon juice: 1 Tbsp (15 ml) is usually enough to give the dish a pleasant acidity. Remove from the heat, fish out the cinnamon stick and citrus peel, season to taste with salt and black pepper and serve piping hot.

Serves 8 as a side dish.

Notes

The spices should be added at the last minute, but you can cook the carrots ahead, up until the stage where the liquid in the pan has reduced to a few tablespoons. Keep the carrots in the pan, covered, then reheat them and stir in the spices.

Herby Potato, Parmesan and Buttermilk Puff

Fresh herbs and tangy cultured buttermilk add zip to this homely dish of baked mashed potatoes. If you're feeling indulgent – and I do hope you are – press big cubes of cold butter into the mixture just before you bake it: your guests will be putty in your hands when they dig in to find a filling of melted sunshine.

2 kg large floury potatoes
about 1¼ cups (310 ml) cultured buttermilk
3 Tbsp (45 ml/45 g) softened butter
1½ cups (375 ml, loosely packed) freshly grated Parmesan or Grana Padano, plus extra for topping
1½ tsp (7.5 ml) baking powder
2 extra-large free-range eggs, lightly whisked
4 Tbsp (60 ml) finely chopped fresh woody herbs of your choice: rosemary, sage, oregano, thyme
salt and milled black pepper
8 x 2-cm-square cubes ice-cold butter
paprika or cayenne pepper for dusting

Heat the oven to 180 °C.

Peel and halve the potatoes and cook them in a large pot of rapidly boiling salted water for 30–40 minutes, or until quite tender, but not falling apart. Drain and mash with 1 cup (250 ml) of buttermilk and the butter until smooth. Allow to cool to lukewarm, then mix in the cheese, baking powder, eggs and herbs. Add just enough of the remaining buttermilk to create a very thick, smooth consistency. Don't over-beat the mixture, or it will become gluey. Season generously with salt and milled black pepper. Tip the mixture into a large greased ovenproof dish, or eight individual dishes. Press the cold butter cubes deep into the mixture. Lightly brush the surface with a little melted butter, sprinkle with a handful of grated Parmesan and dust with paprika. Bake for 20–30 minutes, or until puffed and golden brown.

Serves 8 as a side dish.

Notes

Prepare the dish ready for baking up to 3 hours in advance and keep covered with clingfilm. Don't be tempted to add Cheddar or a similar fatty yellow cheese to this dish, as this will make it unpleasantly oily. To ring the changes, add some cooked, mashed parsnips.

Ricotta-Stuffed Baked Onions with Parmesan Cream

I appreciate a nice baked stuffed onion, but whole ones often seem dauntingly big and aggressively oniony, and I find I seldom finish one. In this dish, I've sliced them in half lengthways and stuffed them with a delicate mixture of ricotta and nutmeg. And then thrown caution to the wind with an indulgent Parmesan cream sauce.

8 large white onions
1 tsp (5 ml) salt
4 Tbsp (60 ml) olive oil
1 Tbsp (15 ml) finely chopped fresh thyme
1 clove garlic, peeled and finely chopped
3 Tbsp (45 ml) dry white wine
½ cup (125 ml) ricotta cheese
2 Tbsp (30 ml) fresh cream
2 pinches (about 2 ml) freshly grated nutmeg
salt and milled black pepper
2 slices white bread, a day or two old
200 ml freshly grated Parmesan

FOR THE SAUCE
1 cup (250 ml) fresh cream
200 ml freshly grated Parmesan
milled black pepper

Put the onions, whole, untrimmed and in their skins, into a large pot and cover with boiling water. Add the salt, bring to the boil and cook at a lively simmer for 15 minutes. Drain in a colander. When cool enough to handle, cut a 3-mm slice off the root end of each onion, peel away the papery casing and cut in half lengthways; that is, from stem to root. Pull out the uncooked centre of each onion half; this should come away quite easily at the point, dividing the 3–5 cooked outer layers and the raw inner ones. Arrange the onion half-shells in a single layer in a large greased baking dish.

Heat the oven to 160 °C. Finely chop the reserved onion centres and fry in 3 Tbsp (45 ml) of olive oil over a medium-low heat for 5 minutes, or until soft and glassy. Stir in the thyme and garlic and cook for another minute. Turn up the heat, add the wine and bubble for a few minutes, or until almost all the liquid has evaporated. Tip into a mixing bowl, add the ricotta, cream and nutmeg and mash with a fork to a smooth paste. Season with salt and pepper, then divide the mixture into 16 portions and use it to stuff the onion shells.

Whizz the bread slices to a fairly fine crumb, add the Parmesan and remaining olive oil and whizz again till well combined. Lightly pat the crumb crust on top of the filled onion shells. Bake for 30–35 minutes, or until the onion shells are very tender and the topping crisp and golden brown.

To make the sauce, gently heat the cream in a small saucepan. When it's about to come to the boil, tip in the Parmesan and whisk until smooth. Bubble gently for another minute or two, until the cheese has melted and the cream has thickened slightly. Season with black pepper (you won't need to add extra salt). Top each baked onion-half with a big dab of Parmesan cream and serve hot.

Serves 8 as a side dish.

Notes

Boil the onions, stuff and top them with the crumb crust up to 4 hours ahead. You can also make the Parmesan cream an hour or two ahead, but cover its surface with a sheet of clingfilm and reheat it very gently just before serving.

Crisp Squashed Potatoes with Tomatoes and Olives

An easy, rustic one-dish bake that can be prepared well in advance, needs little attention and is always polished off in minutes. This is enough to feed eight as a side dish, but you might want to make more if you are feeding a gang of teens or a team of burly rugby players.

10 large floury potatoes
½ cup (125 ml/125 g) butter
6 cloves garlic, peeled and finely grated
juice and finely grated zest of 1 large lemon
20-cm-long branch of fresh rosemary,
leaves stripped
½ cup (125 ml) olive oil
salt and milled black pepper
500 g cherry tomatoes, halved
1 cup (250 ml) calamata olives, pitted

Boil the potatoes, whole and unpeeled, in plenty of generously salted water for about 25 minutes, or until their outer layers are just tender when pierced with a knife, but they are still a little raw on the inside. Drain, cut roughly into 5-cm cubes and spread in a single layer over the base of a large oiled roasting pan (or two smaller ones). Using the back of a fork, lightly squash, rake and scratch the cubes to create a craggy surface. The more surface area you can create, the crisper the potatoes will be. Set the pan aside for an hour or longer so the potatoes can dry out.

Melt the butter and stir in the garlic, lemon juice, zest and half the rosemary leaves. Cool, cover and refrigerate. An hour or so before you serve the dish, set the oven to 190 °C, and melt the flavoured butter. Stir in the olive oil. Using a pastry brush or a baster, generously daub the mixture all over the squashed potatoes. Season with salt and pepper and bake for about 30 minutes, or until the tips of the potatoes are beginning to turn golden. Tuck the halved cherry tomatoes and the remaining rosemary leaves in between the potato crags and bake for another 25 minutes. Scatter the olives over the dish and bake for a further 10 minutes, or until the potatoes are golden and crisp, the tomatoes tender and the olives hot. Season with more salt and pepper, if necessary, and bring the dish to the table piping hot, with a big metal spatula, so your guests can help themselves.

Serves 8 as a side dish.

Notes

The key to achieving a really crisp, golden crust is to allow the potatoes to dry out thoroughly. If you have time, put them, uncovered, in the fridge overnight; the dry air of a fridge works wonders.

Hot Caprese Tart

A classic Italian salad transformed into a 'pizza', albeit one with a base of crisp phyllo pastry. Children who might turn up their noses at a Caprese salad, that sublime combination of ripe tomatoes, milky mozzarella and peppery fresh basil, are surprisingly enthusiastic when they see it presented in a form they know and love. Double this recipe if there are children at the table.

6 sheets phyllo pastry
8 Tbsp (120 ml/120 g) butter
5 Tbsp (75 ml) finely grated Parmesan
8 ripe tomatoes
600 g mozzarella
flaky sea salt and milled black pepper
a small bunch of fresh basil, leaves picked
3 Tbsp (45 ml) olive oil

Heat the oven to 170 °C.

Unroll the phyllo pastry on a board and keep covered with a damp cloth. Melt the butter in a saucepan or the microwave. Start by brushing the bottom and sides of a non-stick baking sheet, then line it with a sheet of phyllo pastry, allowing the edges to drape over the rim. Brush the phyllo layer generously with butter and sprinkle with 1 Tbsp (15 ml) of Parmesan. Add another sheet of phyllo and continue layering, brushing and sprinkling until you have used up all six sheets. Trim any ragged edges and round off the corners with a pair of scissors.

Thinly slice the tomatoes and the mozzarella and arrange the slices, alternately, in overlapping rows on top of the pastry. Sprinkle with salt and pepper. Bake for 10–15 minutes, or until the pastry is crisp and golden, and the cheese melted. Remove from the oven, tuck in the basil leaves and drizzle with the olive oil. Cut into eight squares and serve immediately.

Serves 8 as a starter or side dish.

Notes

Prepare the phyllo pastry base up to 6 hours in advance, but cover it tightly with several sheets of clingfilm so it doesn't dry out. Slice the cheese and keep covered. The tomatoes should be sliced at the last minute.

Spinach, Egg and Three-Cheese Phyllo Pie

This substantial dish is, of course, a Greek spanakopita, but I've given it extra pizzazz with whole baked eggs, toasted pine nuts, dill and sesame seeds. Lovely hot or cold, with a homemade tomato sauce or dollops of tzatziki.

350 g fresh spinach or Swiss chard, stalks removed
4 Tbsp (60 ml) pine nuts
1 large onion, peeled and finely chopped
3 Tbsp (45 ml) olive oil
2 cloves garlic, peeled and finely chopped
150 g feta cheese, crumbled
150 g ricotta cheese
6 Tbsp (90 ml) finely grated Parmesan, plus extra for dusting
juice and finely grated zest of 1 lemon
¼ of a whole nutmeg, finely grated
4 Tbsp (60 ml) finely chopped fresh dill (optional)
10 extra-large free-range eggs
salt and milled black pepper
8 sheets phyllo pastry
olive oil or melted butter for brushing
1 Tbsp (15 ml) sesame or poppy seeds

Rinse the spinach and place it, water still clinging to its leaves, in a large pot. Cook over a high heat, turning often, for 6–7 minutes, until the leaves have wilted right down. Drain in a colander and, when the spinach is cool enough to handle, patiently squeeze out as much liquid as you can by pressing it between your palms to a tightly compressed lump about the size of a tennis ball. Place on a board and use a sharp knife to chop it very finely.

Place the pine nuts in a dry frying pan and toss over a low heat until lightly toasted. Reserve. Fry the onion gently in the olive oil for 5–6 minutes, or until soft and glassy. Stir in the garlic and cook for another minute. Tip the onion into a large mixing bowl, cool for 5 minutes and add the chopped spinach, pine nuts, feta, ricotta, Parmesan, lemon juice, zest, nutmeg and dill (if you're using it). Lightly whisk 2 eggs and stir them into the mixture. Season to taste with salt and pepper.

Heat the oven to 190 °C. Grease a large rectangular baking dish and line it with a sheet of phyllo pastry. Brush the base and sides of the sheet with olive oil or melted butter and dust with a little Parmesan. Place another sheet on top, and continue layering, brushing and dusting until you have used four sheets in total. Pile the filling into the pastry and smooth the surface. Make eight deep hollows in the filling, evenly spaced across the dish, and carefully break 1 egg into each one. Place another sheet of phyllo on top and continue brushing with oil and dusting with Parmesan until you have used up the remaining sheets. Tuck the edges neatly down the sides of the dish and use a knife to lightly mark the pie into portions, ensuring that each portion has an egg. Generously brush the surface with oil or butter and sprinkle with sesame or poppy seeds. Bake for 30–40 minutes, or until the pastry is crisp and golden brown. Serve hot or cold.

Serves 8 as a side dish.

Notes

This pie can be prepared up to 6 hours ahead. Keep the phyllo pastry covered with clingfilm to prevent it from drying out. If you're in a hurry, use a can of spray-on olive oil to grease the phyllo sheets. If you can't find fresh dill, use parsley.

Cheese, Onion and Green Olive Tart

A rich savoury tart that is among my all-time favourites. This dish is adapted from a recipe given to my mother by a dear friend over forty years ago, and it's one of those classics that never disappoints. It contains both raw grated onion and an indecent amount of grated Cheddar, and that's why it tastes so fantastic. If you're serving this as a main course, double the quantities and make two tarts.

FOR THE PASTRY SHELL
250 g cake flour
a pinch of salt
150 g cold butter, cubed
2 egg yolks
iced water

FOR THE FILLING
4 extra-large free-range eggs, lightly whisked
450 g Cheddar cheese, grated
1 onion, peeled and finely grated
½ cup (125 ml) milk
½ cup (125 ml) fresh cream
3 Tbsp (45 ml) finely chopped fresh parsley
1 Tbsp (15 ml) finely chopped fresh thyme
salt and milled black pepper
12 pimento-stuffed green olives
2 tsp (10 ml) poppy seeds

Heat the oven to 180 °C.

To make the pastry shell, sift the flour and salt into a bowl and add the butter. Using your fingertips, rub the butter into the flour until the mixture resembles fine breadcrumbs. (Or blitz in a food processor fitted with a metal blade.) Add the egg yolks and just enough iced water to form a light, crumbly dough. Pat into a circle, wrap in clingfilm and rest in the fridge for 20 minutes. Roll out the pastry and use it to line a greased 23-cm flan dish. Prick the bottom of the pastry shell and bake blind (p. 165).

For the filling, lightly whisk the eggs in a mixing bowl. Stir in the cheese, onion, milk, cream and herbs and season with salt and pepper. Tip the filling into the pastry shell. Cut the stuffed olives in half crossways and press, cut-side up, into the surface of the tart. Sprinkle the top with poppy seeds and bake for 35–40 minutes, or until puffed and lightly browned on top, but with a slight wobble in the centre. Serve warm, with a green salad.

Serves 8 as a side dish or starter.

Notes

This can be served cold, but it's best warm, so prepare the filling and blind bake the pastry in advance, then fill the pie and bake it an hour or so before you serve it. If you can't be bothered with rolling and blind baking pastry, simply press it straight into the pie dish and add the filling. The base will be somewhat soggy, but I don't think anyone will notice.

Buttery Tomato Tart

This intensely flavoured, summery tomato sauce contains a scandalous amount of butter, but it's worth every calorie. You can use any creamy, soft white cheese, but avoid pungent goat's milk cheeses. Steer clear of rocket too, because its aggressive pepperiness will overwhelm the star ingredient.

8 Tbsp (120 ml/120 g) butter
2 tsp (10 ml) olive oil
1 kg ripe, sweet cherry tomatoes
2 thumb-length sprigs fresh rosemary
1 sprig fresh thyme
1 large clove garlic, peeled and finely chopped
a pinch of chilli flakes (optional)
salt and milled black pepper
6 Tbsp (90 ml) fresh cream
2 x 400 g rolls readymade puff pastry, thawed
1 beaten egg, for brushing

FOR TOPPING
150 g mild, creamy white cheese, such as feta
a handful of fresh baby herb leaves: oregano, marjoram or basil

Heat the butter and oil in a large pan and add the whole tomatoes and herb sprigs. Cook, tossing often, over a medium-high heat, for 5 minutes, or until the tomatoes have softened slightly. Using a potato masher, lightly crush the tomatoes to release their juices. Add the garlic and chilli flakes and season with salt and pepper. Turn up the heat and cook at a vigorous bubble for 5 minutes, or until the sauce has thickened and reduced slightly. Stir in the cream and bubble for another minute. Discard the herb sprigs and keep warm.

Set the oven to 180 °C and heat two baking sheets. Unroll each puff pastry cylinder onto a sheet of baking paper. Lightly roll out the pastry to increase its size by about 2 cm on all sides. Using a sharp knife, trim a 1-cm-wide strip off each edge. Brush the pastry with beaten egg and prick all over with a fork. Place the strips of pastry around the edges of the rectangle to form a raised border. Mark a chevron pattern on the border, using a knife. Brush the borders with egg. Cut out two rectangles of foil exactly the same size as the base (measure by placing the foil over the pastry and running your thumbnail around the inside edge of the border). Place the foil on top of the pastry. Lift the pastry sheets, on their paper, and place them on the hot baking sheets (you may need another pair of hands for this). Bake for 10 minutes, then remove the foil and bake for a further 10–15 minutes, or until the pastry is golden and crisp. Don't worry if the middle of the pastry puffs up; it will soon subside.

Peel off the foil and place the bases on wire racks so the bottoms remain crisp. Just before you serve the tarts, spread the warm tomato sauce over the bases. Scatter with small chunks of cheese and a sprinkling of baby herb leaves. Slice into squares and serve immediately.

Serves 8 as a snack.

Notes | The pastry bases can be prepared, ready for cooking, up to 8 hours in advance and kept covered in the fridge. Bring the pastry up to room temperature before it goes into the oven. Prepare the tomato sauce up to 24 hours in advance and warm it gently before spreading it over the pastry.

Moroccan-Spiced Lentils with Roast Cherry Tomatoes

Packed with the singing flavours of North Africa, this versatile dish can be served cold or warm as a salad, or piping hot as a side dish. I've specified feta cheese, but you can use any suitable white cheese here: it's also very good with goat's milk cheese, lightly fried halloumi or Greek kefalotyri.

500 g ripe cherry tomatoes
3 Tbsp (45 ml) olive oil
salt and milled black pepper
2 cups (500 ml) brown lentils
1 stick of cinnamon
1 tsp (5 ml) caraway seeds (optional)
4 cups (1 litre) warm water
1 cup (250 ml) whole green olives, pitted
3 Tbsp (45 ml) finely chopped preserved lemon (see Notes)
1½ cups (375 ml) crumbled feta cheese
½ cup (125 ml) chopped fresh coriander

FOR THE DRESSING
⅔ cup (160 ml) olive oil
⅓ cup (80 ml) balsamic vinegar
juice of 1 lemon
2 cloves garlic, peeled and crushed
4 tsp (20 ml) dried mint
1 tsp (5 ml) dried red chilli flakes
2 tsp (10 ml) ground cumin
½ tsp (2.5 ml) ground cinnamon
½ tsp (2.5 ml) paprika

Heat the oven to 160 °C.

Toss the cherry tomatoes in olive oil, season with salt and pepper, place in a ceramic dish and bake, undisturbed, for 1 hour, or until collapsed. Rinse the lentils, place in a pot with the cinnamon stick and caraway seeds and cover with water. Bring to the boil and simmer for 30 minutes, or until almost all the water has been absorbed and the lentils are cooked through, but not mushy. Drain and place in a large bowl. Discard the cinnamon stick. Add the green olives, preserved lemon and warm roast tomatoes.

To make the dressing, place all the ingredients in a bowl and whisk well to combine. Pour the dressing over the lentils and toss gently. Season generously with salt and pepper. Just before serving, sprinkle over the crumbled feta and chopped coriander.

Serves 8 as a salad or side dish.

Notes

This can be made a day ahead and kept covered in the fridge, but add the cheese and coriander at the last minute. If you can't find preserved lemons in your local deli, use the finely grated zest of a small lemon instead.

Spicy Chickpea, Pepper and Sausage Stew

If you have a tight budget, this is a good choice for a feast because it stretches eight sausages into a satisfying rib-sticker of a dish. I think sausages (or at least some crisped bacon) are essential to create an unctuous, well-flavoured sauce, but leave them out of a portion of the stew if there are vegetarians at the table.

8 medium potatoes
3 Tbsp (45 ml) olive or sunflower oil
1 large onion, peeled and finely chopped
3 stalks celery (no leaves), sliced
2 red peppers, sliced
1 red chilli, deseeded and finely chopped
3 cloves garlic, peeled and finely grated
½ tsp (2.5 ml) salt
8 pork sausages
2 Tbsp (30 ml) balsamic or malt vinegar
4 Tbsp (60 ml) tomato sauce
2 x 400 g tins chopped Italian tomatoes
2 tsp (10 ml) Tabasco sauce, or to taste
¾ cup (180 ml) dry white wine
2 tsp (10 ml) ground cumin
1½ tsp (7.5 ml) paprika
2 x 400 g tins chickpeas, drained
milled black pepper
chopped fresh parsley or coriander for serving
1 x 200 g tub tzatziki (optional)

Peel the potatoes and cut each into six pieces. Cook in plenty of rapidly boiling salted water for about 12 minutes, or until almost cooked through.

In the meantime, heat the oil in a large pan (a big wok is ideal), add the onion, celery and red peppers and fry, over a medium-high heat, for 7 minutes, or until just soft. Add the chilli, garlic and salt and cook for another minute, without allowing the garlic to brown. Tip onto a plate and set aside.

Add the sausages to the same pan and fry for 6–7 minutes on all sides, or until their skins are brown and burnished. Drain the excess fat, leaving the sausages in the pan, and use a pair of kitchen scissors to snip each sausage into three pieces. Return the cooked vegetables to the pan and turn up the heat. Add the vinegar and stir briskly to loosen any sediment on the bottom of the pan. Stir in the tomato sauce, tinned tomatoes, Tabasco, white wine, cumin, paprika and chickpeas. Cook at a lively bubble, stirring occasionally, for 10 minutes.

Drain the potatoes and add them to the stew, along with a ladleful or two of the boiling water in which you cooked them – just enough to create a rich gravy. Turn down the heat and simmer for a further 5 minutes, adding more hot water if necessary. Season generously with pepper and more salt if required. Serve hot, topped with chopped fresh parsley or coriander and a dollop of cold tzatziki.

Serves 8.

Notes

This can be made a day ahead and kept covered in the fridge. If you're reserving a sausageless portion for vegetarian guests, bake the sausages in a hot oven and add them to the stew after the chickpeas go in. This is also good with sliced chorizo sausage.

Lentil and Butternut Bobotie

This mildly spiced dish is so comforting and full of flavour that I actually prefer it to a classic mince-based bobotie. To be a perfect feast dish, however, it must be served with a nostalgic selection of the sambals that were once considered essential to a Seventies-style South African curry: sliced bananas, desiccated coconut, 'hotters' made with finely chopped onions and tomatoes, and, of course, dollops of Mrs Ball's chutney.

2 butternuts (about 1 kg) with small bulbs and long slim necks
olive oil
salt and milled black pepper
2 onions, peeled and finely chopped
1½ cups (375 ml) brown lentils
1 stick of cinnamon
3 cups (750 ml) vegetable stock or water
1 x 400 g tin chopped Italian tomatoes
3 cloves garlic, peeled and finely grated
2 Tbsp (30 ml) finely grated fresh ginger
½ cup (125 ml) chopped dried peaches or apricots
½ cup (125 ml) sultanas
⅔ cup (160 ml) raw almonds, very coarsely chopped
3 Tbsp (45 ml) smooth apricot jam
1 Tbsp (15 ml) medium-strength curry powder
2 tsp (10 ml) ground cumin
1 tsp (5 ml) ground coriander
juice of 1 small lemon
3 extra-large free-range eggs
1 cup (250 ml) milk
½ tsp (2.5 ml) turmeric
fresh lemon or bay leaves, or both

Heat the oven to 180 °C.

Slice the necks of the butternuts – without peeling them – into 1-cm-thick discs. (Keep the seed-filled bulbs of the butternut for another dish.) Arrange on an oiled baking sheet, smear generously with olive oil and season with salt and pepper. Bake for 40–50 minutes, or until very soft but not collapsed. Arrange the slices in a single layer on the base of a greased ovenproof dish.

In the meantime, make the filling. Fry the onions over a medium heat in 4 Tbsp (60 ml) of olive oil until they're soft and a light golden colour. Add the lentils, cinnamon stick and vegetable stock and simmer briskly, uncovered, for 30 minutes, or until almost all the liquid has evaporated. Stir in the tomatoes, garlic and ginger and cook gently for another 10 minutes, or until the lentils are just soft and the mixture has thickened slightly (it should still be moist, but on no account sloppy). Remove the cinnamon stick and stir in the peaches, sultanas, almonds, jam, spices and lemon juice. Season generously with salt and pepper, pour the mixture over the butternut slices and press down lightly so the surface is level.

In a separate bowl, lightly whisk the eggs, milk and turmeric together. Season with salt and pepper and gently trickle the mixture over the lentils. Press a few fresh lemon or bay leaves into the egg topping and bake for 25–30 minutes, or until the custard has set. Serve immediately with steaming hot Basmati rice and a selection of sambals.

Serves 8.

Notes	This can be made up to 36 hours ahead and kept covered in the fridge, but mix and pour over the custard topping no more than 2 hours before you bake it.

Pappardelle with Mushrooms, Crème Fraîche and Rosemary

The word 'pappardelle' is derived from the Italian 'gobble it up', and that's just what your guests will do when they dive into this simple but utterly luxurious dish of pasta ribbons cloaked in a creamy mushroom sauce (photo, p. 52). This is easy to make, but follow the steps in the recipe closely so the mushrooms have a chance to absorb the garlic, rosemary and red-wine flavours before the crème fraîche is added.

2 Tbsp (30 ml) butter
2 Tbsp (30 ml) olive oil
5 slim leeks, white and pale green parts only, finely sliced
4 punnets (1 kg) portabellini or mixed mushrooms, sliced
1 x 10-cm-long branch of fresh rosemary
3 cloves garlic, peeled and finely grated
½ tsp (2.5 ml) dried red chilli flakes (optional)
salt and milled black pepper
6 Tbsp (90 ml) red wine
1½ cups (375 ml) water or vegetable stock
2 tubs (about 500 ml) crème fraîche
lemon juice
750 g pappardelle or similar flat pasta

FOR TOPPING
1 x 150 g wedge of Parmesan or Grana Padano
sprigs of fresh chervil or a handful of finely chopped fresh parsley

Heat the butter and oil in a very large, shallow pan (an electric frying pan is ideal), add the leeks and sauté over a medium heat for 3–5 minutes, or until the leeks are soft (do not allow them to brown). Add the mushrooms, rosemary, garlic, chilli flakes and a large pinch of salt and cook, stirring occasionally, for 6–8 minutes, or until you see liquid collecting at the bottom of the pan. Pour in the wine, turn up the heat and cook at a brisk bubble for a further 5–6 minutes, or until almost all the liquid in the pan has evaporated, leaving a slightly syrupy glaze. Add the water and crème fraîche, stir briskly to combine, turn down the heat again and simmer for 10 minutes, or until the sauce has reduced slightly and is thick and creamy. Fish out the rosemary branch and season the mushroom mixture generously with black pepper and more salt, if necessary. Add a spritz of lemon juice – you'll need just enough to give the sauce a little fresh zing. If the sauce seems too thick to coat the pasta, thin it to the desired consistency with warm water. At this point, you can set the sauce aside, covered, for up to 8 hours.

When it's time to serve, reheat the sauce over a gentle heat and place a large platter in the oven to warm. Cook the pappardelle in plenty of salted boiling water for 9–10 minutes, or until *al dente*. Drain the pasta, pile it onto the warmed platter and pour over the mushroom sauce. Using a potato peeler, shave thin flakes of Parmesan all over the top, scatter with fresh chervil leaves or chopped parsley and serve immediately, with a green salad.

Serves 8.

Notes

The secret to perfect pasta is to cook it in a great volume of rapidly boiling salted water for the exact time specified on the packet, and to drain it very briefly. Pasta that is left to stand in a colander for too long quickly becomes sticky and dry, so drain it for no longer than 30 seconds and pile it onto the platter while it's still ever so slightly damp.

Ricotta-Filled Paccheri with a Tomato Butter Sauce

The defining deliciousness of this sunny baked pasta dish comes from a sauce made from just a few ingredients: burstingly ripe cherry tomatoes cooked to stickiness in a lot of hot butter, then lightly mashed with a whisper of garlic, shredded fresh sage and a splash of cream. A somewhat fiddly dish, but well worth the effort.

650 g large pasta tubes (paccheri or similar)
1 kg ripe cherry tomatoes
8 Tbsp (120 ml/120 g) butter
1 Tbsp (15 ml) olive oil
4 cloves garlic, peeled and finely chopped
10 fresh sage leaves, finely shredded
½ cup (125 ml) fresh cream
salt and milled black pepper
¾ cup (180 ml) freshly grated Parmesan

FOR THE STUFFING
2 onions, peeled and very finely chopped
2 Tbsp (30 ml) light olive or sunflower oil
1 Tbsp (15 ml/15 g) butter
1 cup (250 ml, loosely packed) finely chopped flat-leaf parsley
2 Tbsp (30 ml) freshly squeezed lemon juice
550 g ricotta cheese, crumbled
2 extra-large free-range eggs
¼ of a whole nutmeg, finely grated
salt and milled black pepper
about 5 Tbsp (75 ml) fresh cream
2 cups (500 ml) hot water

First make the stuffing. Fry the onions in the oil and butter over a medium-low heat for 4 minutes, or until soft and transparent. Cool for a few minutes, then place in a bowl and stir in the parsley, lemon juice, ricotta, eggs and nutmeg. Season with salt and pepper. Now add just enough cream to turn the mixture into a fairly slack paste that can easily be squeezed through the nozzle of a piping bag.

Butter a deep (at least 15 cm) ceramic or glass baking dish big enough to hold all the pasta tubes standing upright (or use two smaller dishes). Place a pasta tube upright on a chopping board and, using a piping bag, fill it three-quarters of the way to the top with the ricotta mixture. Pack the tubes upright in the dish, leaning them against the sides to begin with. Trickle the water down the sides of the dish so that the bottoms of the tubes are submerged.

For the sauce, cut a small slash in each cherry tomato. Heat the butter and olive oil in a large shallow pan, add the tomatoes and cook, over a high heat, tossing often, for 7–10 minutes, or until the tomatoes begin to brown and a sticky golden residue forms on the bottom of the pan. Stir in the garlic and shredded sage and, using a potato masher, lightly crush the tomatoes. Turn down the heat and simmer very gently for another 7–10 minutes, or until slightly thickened, crushing the tomatoes now and again to release their juices. Stir in the cream and season to taste with salt and pepper. Pour the sauce over the pasta tubes, without stirring. Give the dish a gentle shake, cover with clingfilm and set aside for 1 hour.

Heat the oven to 170 °C. Sprinkle the dish with grated Parmesan and bake for 35–45 minutes, or until the pasta is tender and the sauce bubbling vigorously. Serve immediately with fresh rocket or mixed salad leaves.

Serves 8.

Notes

This dish can be assembled up to 6 hours in advance (and you can make the tomato sauce the day before, then warm it slightly before you pour it over the tubes). Don't skip the standing time, or the tubes will not absorb enough liquid to cook properly. If you run out of stuffing before the dish is full, put a few empty pasta tubes between the full ones so that the dish is fairly tightly packed.

Linguine with a Chilled Sauce of Chicken, Tomato and Herbs

I love contrasts of hot and cold, crunchy and smooth, and this dish of cold, zingy sauce poured over slippery hot pasta is among my all-time favourite recipes. My method of oven-poaching chicken results in perfectly tender and succulent breasts every time; try it and you'll never go back to cooking them on the stovetop. This is excellent hot and cold, but equally delicious served as a pasta salad, at room temperature.

8 deboned, skinless chicken breasts
2 bay leaves
½ onion stuck with 2 whole cloves
4 stalks parsley
1 thin slice of lemon
1 tsp (5 ml) salt
milled black pepper
hot water
1½ packets (750 g) linguine
1½ cups (375 ml) peppered or plain feta cheese

FOR THE SAUCE

1 cup (250 ml) flat-leaf parsley leaves
1 cup (250 ml) basil leaves
1 kg ripe cherry tomatoes, thickly sliced
6 spring onions, white and pale green parts only, finely sliced
3 cloves garlic, peeled and finely grated
4 Tbsp (60 ml) white wine vinegar
1 cup (250 ml) extra-virgin olive oil
1 tsp (5 ml) white sugar
½ tsp (2.5 ml) dried red chilli flakes, or more, to taste
1 cup (250 ml) olives of your choice, pitted (optional)

Heat the oven to 180 °C.

Arrange the chicken breasts in a single layer in a ceramic or glass baking dish and add the bay leaves, onion, parsley, lemon slice, salt and six grinds of the peppermill. Pour over just enough hot water to cover the breasts. Place in the oven and poach for 25–30 minutes, or until the breasts are just cooked through (see Notes). Cover the dish and allow the breasts to cool to lukewarm in their liquid (refrigerate if you're not going to use them within an hour or two).

In the meantime make the sauce. Finely chop half the parsley and basil leaves, place in a mixing bowl and add the tomatoes, spring onions, garlic, vinegar, olive oil, sugar and chilli flakes. Gently mix everything together, cover and set aside until the chicken breasts have cooled. Remove the breasts from their poaching liquid, tear into strips the size of your pinkie finger and add to the bowl. Stir in ½ cup (125 ml) of the cooled poaching liquid. Season to taste with salt and pepper and toss well. Cover and chill for at least 30 minutes (or up to 2 hours; see Notes) to allow the flavours to mingle and the chicken to soak up the dressing.

When you're ready to serve, cook the linguine in plenty of rapidly boiling salted water for 9–10 minutes, or until *al dente*. Drain the pasta for 30 seconds and tip it onto a large platter. Tear up the remaining basil and parsley leaves and stir them and the olives into the sauce. Heap the cold sauce on top of the hot pasta, scatter with feta, drizzle over a little more olive oil and serve immediately.

Serves 8.

Notes

How long the chicken breasts will take to cook to perfection depends on their size. Check for doneness after 25 minutes by cutting a slit in the thick part of one of the breasts; if there's any pinkness, cook for a few more minutes. The breasts can be poached the day before and refrigerated, but make the sauce no more than 2 hours before you cook the pasta, or it will lose its fresh zip. Save the leftover poaching liquid for a soup or stew.

Spaghettini with Creamy Onion, Lemon and Caviar Sauce

Very special occasions deserve special food, and this simple yet indulgent pasta dish perfectly fits the bill. The important thing here is to achieve a silken, unctuous sauce, so be sure to use a top-quality full-fat cream cheese: the low-fat variety, or creamed cottage cheese, will not do. Good black lumpfish roe or caviar is expensive, but it goes a long way, and adds an essential, delicate ocean taste to this sauce.

2 x 250 g tubs full-fat cream cheese
4 Tbsp (60 ml/60 g) butter
2 medium onions, peeled and very finely and neatly diced
2 small cloves garlic, peeled and crushed
5 Tbsp (75 ml) dry white wine
juice of 1 large lemon
1 Tbsp (15 ml) finely grated lemon zest
1½ cups (375 ml) fresh cream
1½ packets (750 g) spaghettini or similar thin pasta
1 x 100 g tub good-quality black lumpfish roe

Place the cream cheese in a large mixing bowl and beat energetically with a metal whisk until smooth and creamy. Set aside.

Melt the butter in a large, shallow pan, add the onions and garlic and cover their surface with a circle of baking paper, or the wrapper from a block of butter. Cook over a very low heat for 10 minutes, or until the onions are translucent and soft. Remove the paper, turn up the heat slightly and add the wine and lemon juice. Bubble briskly for 3 minutes, or until the liquid in the pan has reduced to a tablespoon or so of slightly sticky glaze. Turn the heat down again, add the cream cheese and whisk until smooth. Add the lemon zest and cream and bubble gently for a further 2–3 minutes, stirring all the time. If the sauce seems a little too thick to coat the spaghettini (this will depend on the type of cream cheese you've used) thin it with a few tablespoons of warm water; it should be about the consistency of pouring cream. Cover the pan and set aside.

When you're ready to serve, cook the pasta in plenty of rapidly boiling salted water for 9–10 minutes, or until *al dente*. Put eight pasta bowls in a low oven to warm. While the pasta's cooking, gently reheat the sauce till very hot, but don't let it boil. Drain the pasta for 30 seconds in a colander, then tip it, still slightly damp, into the hot sauce. Remove from the heat, add 2–3 Tbsp (30–45 ml, or more, to taste) of the caviar and gently toss together so every strand of pasta is coated. Swirl the spaghettini into the warmed bowls and top each one with a little extra caviar. Serve with a plain salad of mixed dark green leaves dressed with olive oil, lemon juice and salt.

Serves 8.

Notes

The sauce, hot pasta and lumpfish roe must be tossed together immediately before serving, but you can make the sauce — up to the point where you thin it with water — well in advance. Keep it in a lidded container in the fridge, then reheat it and continue with the recipe.

Seafood

Fish, crustaceans and molluscs taken straight from the earth's clean oceans are the only wild, untainted foods still freely available to us as consumers, but they come at a cost. Several costs, in fact, and some of them steep. First, seafood is a somewhat tricky choice for a family feast. Most children don't like it (except disguised as fingers coated with orange crumbs) and many adults are iffy about it too. A surprising number of people have a genuine aversion to bony fish, and that's why I never serve a whole fish at an important meal. It's not much of a feast, I reckon, if your guests are fretting about getting a bone lodged in their throats. It's also difficult to portion a whole fish neatly — the plates always end up looking as if cats have been fighting over them. If you're determined to serve a whole fish, choose a big meaty one with a rugged skeleton — three or four small flappers bristling with tiny bones will not be a hit with guests. Or go for fat steaks or cutlets cut from a large, firm-textured fish; there's less risk of lurking bones, and the portions will look trim and tempting on the plate.

Second, I think there's little point in buying frozen linefish — it's astonishingly expensive and loses texture, taste and springiness in the freezer. If you can't find spanking-fresh, sustainable fish at your local fishmonger or supermarket, I recommend that you abandon the idea of fish altogether. You can, however, get away with frozen calamari (p. 50) and mussels, provided they are of top quality.

Third, it's worth considering, when you plan a feast involving seafood, that cooking fish to perfection requires split-second timing, and that this isn't easy to achieve when you're running around filling glasses and scraping plates. Fish is unforgiving. Unlike chicken or red meat, it can't be left to loll about 'resting' on a plate while you attend to last-minute vegetable and salad details. For this reason I've designed the recipes in this chapter so they can be made well in advance, or require just a few minutes' concentrated attention at the last moment.

Finally, and most important, there are only so many fish in the sea. All these recipes use sustainable seafood and comply with the South African Sustainable Seafood Initiative (SASSI). I was keen to include all sorts of ocean creatures in this chapter until a conversation with an old friend who is a marine biologist and environmental activist opened my eyes to the havoc caused by the irresponsible plundering of fragile fish species both locally and worldwide. My advice is to ask your fishmonger about which sustainable fish is best for each of these dishes. If he hasn't acquainted himself with the issues (and a worrying number of fishmongers haven't), consult the SASSI website (www.wwfsassi.co.za).

Smoked Snoek Chowder

Smoked snoek is usually relegated to dips and pâtés, but I think this prince among South African ingredients deserves to play a starring role. If you can't find snoek in a supermarket, ask your fishmonger to order it for you. This mildly smoky, creamy chowder is quick and easy to make and so flavoursome it really doesn't need a fish stock.

700 g oak-smoked snoek
6 medium leeks, white and pale green parts only
6 Tbsp (90 ml/90 g) butter
2 large sprigs of fresh thyme
1 bay leaf
2 cloves garlic, peeled and crushed
100 ml cake flour
1.5 litres full-cream milk
900 ml water
½ cup (125 ml) dry white wine
salt
8 large floury potatoes, peeled and cut into 2-cm cubes
a pinch or two of white pepper
juice of 1 lemon
½ cup (125 ml) finely chopped flat-leaf parsley or snipped chives

Remove the skin and bones from the snoek and flake the flesh into a bowl. With your fingertips, painstakingly sift through the fish for any small bones you might have missed. Make a lengthways slit halfway through the leeks, rinse the inner leaves under running water to remove any grit, and cut into fine slices. Melt the butter in a large pot, add the leeks, thyme sprigs and bay leaf, cover their surface with a circle of baking paper (or the wrapper from a block of butter) and cook over a very low heat for 7–9 minutes, or until soft. Remove the paper, stir in the garlic and flour and cook for another minute.

Turn up the heat. Combine the milk, water and wine in a jug and pour the liquid into the pot, stirring briskly to disperse any lumps. Add half the flaked snoek, season with salt and, stirring all the time, bring to a gentle boil. Add the potato cubes, turn down the heat and cook at a gentle bubble for about 25 minutes, or until the potato cubes are cooked through but not falling apart. Add the remaining snoek and heat through for 5 minutes. Season with a little white pepper and more salt if necessary. Remove the thyme sprigs and bay leaf.

Stir in the lemon juice and serve hot, with a dusting of parsley or a handful of snipped chives.

Serves 8.

Notes

You can prepare the chowder a day ahead, but reheat the soup gently so the potato cubes stay intact. If you're cubing the potatoes ahead, cover them with cold water to which you have added a squeeze of lemon juice. Don't worry if the soup looks a little thin to begin with: the potato cubes will thicken it up. (And if it's too thick at the end of cooking, thin with a little milk or stock.)

Spicy Fish Pie with Coriander Mash

There are those who dislike fish pie because it reminds them of boarding school, but they may very well be swayed by my curried version, with its rich and perfumed coconut-milk gravy. This is quite mildly spiced, so feel free to warm it up by adding fresh or dried chillies. You can get away with using frozen shrimps, but only spanking-fresh fish will do.

1.5 kg firm-textured white linefish
4 Tbsp (60 ml) sunflower oil
2 tsp (10 ml) mustard seeds
4 white cardamom pods
1 small stick of cinnamon
8 dried curry leaves or 6 fresh ones
2 large onions, peeled and finely chopped
600 ml coconut milk
6 Tbsp (90 ml) water
2½ tsp (12.5 ml) ground cumin
2 tsp (10 ml) medium-strength curry powder
1 Tbsp (15 ml) cornflour
4 Tbsp (60 ml) finely chopped flat-leaf parsley
4 Tbsp (60 ml) fresh cream
salt and milled black pepper

FOR THE MARINADE
juice of 1 lemon
4 cloves garlic, peeled and finely grated
2 Tbsp (30 ml) finely grated fresh ginger
1 tsp (5 ml) chilli powder
1 tsp (5 ml) turmeric
1 tsp (5 ml) salt

FOR THE MASH
12 large potatoes, peeled
milk and butter for mashing
¾ cup (180 ml) chopped fresh coriander

Skin the fish, remove all the bones and cut it into large (about 4 cm) cubes. Mix the marinade ingredients together in a large bowl, add the fish chunks and toss everything together so each piece is coated. Cover and marinate for 20 minutes while you make the sauce.

Heat the oven to 190 °C. Heat the oil in a large pan, add the mustard seeds, cardamom, cinnamon and curry leaves and fry for 1 minute, or until the seeds begin to crackle. Add the onions, turn down the heat a little and cook for 4–5 minutes, or until soft and golden (don't allow the onions to scorch). Now stir in the coconut milk, water, cumin and curry powder, turn down the heat and cook at a brisk bubble for 10 minutes, or until the sauce has thickened slightly. Add the fish cubes and their marinade and bubble very gently for 3 minutes, shaking the pan now and then. Slake the cornflour in a little lemon juice, add it to the sauce and stir gently over a low heat until the sauce has thickened. If it seems too thin, add a little more cornflour (the sauce should thickly coat the back of a spoon). Stir in the parsley and cream and season generously with salt and pepper. Taste the sauce and add a spritz of lemon juice if you feel it needs sharpening. Remove the cinnamon stick and tip the mixture into a large, shallow ovenproof dish, or eight smaller ones.

To make the mash, cut up the potatoes and cook until tender in plenty of boiling salted water. Drain the cubes and mash them with a little butter and milk until smooth and fluffy. Season lavishly with salt and pepper and stir in the coriander. Pile the mash on top of the fish, spreading it gently right to the edges of the dish to form a seal. Rake the top of the mash with a fork and brush with a little melted butter.

Bake for 25–35 minutes, or until the top is golden. Serve with a green salad.

Serves 8.

Notes

The fish pie can be assembled 2 hours ahead, and you can make the sauce (without adding the marinated fish) a day ahead. Don't marinate the fish for too long, or it will become mushy. Ring the changes by adding hard-boiled eggs, mussels or small calamari rings to the sauce.

Libyan Spiced Fish

This colourful, aromatic dish, known as *h'raimeh* or *hraimi*, and consisting of fish pieces poached in a spicy tomato gravy, is found in different forms across the Maghreb. It's popular in Israel too, where it was introduced by North African Jews and is known as *chreime*. There are many variations of this recipe, and in my adaptation I've used a sticky reduction of cherry tomatoes to give the sauce body and intensity.

½ cup (125 ml) olive oil
2 large onions, peeled and very finely chopped
500 g ripe cherry tomatoes
6 cloves garlic, peeled and finely grated
1 tsp (5 ml) caraway seeds, ground to a powder
2 tsp (10 ml) ground cumin
1 Tbsp (15 ml) paprika
1 tsp (5 ml) dried red chilli flakes, or more, to taste
2 cups (500 ml) warm water
5 Tbsp (75 ml) lemon juice
salt and milled black pepper
8 x 250 g pieces of firm-textured fish, such as dorado or yellowtail
½ cup (125 ml) chopped fresh coriander

Heat the oil in a shallow pan (it should be large enough to hold all the fish pieces in a single layer) and add the onions. Fry over a medium heat for 3 minutes, without allowing them to brown. Put the cherry tomatoes in a liquidiser and press the pulse button a few times to break them up to a rough, chunky texture (or finely chop them with a knife). Turn the heat up to its maximum, throw in the tomatoes and cook, stirring often, for 7–8 minutes, or until the sauce is thick and sticky, and the oil begins to separate. Turn down the heat, stir in the garlic, caraway, cumin, paprika and chilli flakes and cook for another minute. Add the water and lemon juice and season with salt and pepper. Bubble the sauce fairly briskly for 10 minutes, or until slightly reduced and thickened. If it seems too thick, thin it with a little water. At this point, you can set the sauce aside until you're ready to poach the fish.

Season the fish pieces and place them in a single layer in the sauce. Cook them for 2½–3 minutes on one side, then flip them over and cook for a further 3 minutes. How long the fish pieces will take to cook depends on their thickness; check for doneness by poking the tip of a knife into the thickest part of the biggest fillet (see also Notes; p. 100).

Arrange the fillets on a warm platter (or on individual plates) and pour over the sauce. Scatter with coriander and serve immediately, with couscous, a couscous salad (p. 150) or a pile of sliced crusty bread.

Serves 8.

Notes | Don't take your eye off the fish while it's poaching: 2 minutes too long and its texture will be ruined. Make the sauce up to 24 hours ahead. You can use harissa paste or fresh chillies in place of the chilli flakes, but don't omit the caraway, which gives the dish a distinctive fragrance.

Salmon, Egg and Dill Pie with Lemon Butter

This homely pie is similar to traditional Russian coulibiac or kulebyáka, but I like to think of it as a kedgeree-in-pastry, as it has all the elements that make that famous Anglo-Indian dish so tempting: soft flakes of fish, boiled eggs, creamy rice and plenty of fresh parsley and dill, with a tingle of black and cayenne pepper. A fine dish for a feast.

¾ cup (180 ml) uncooked long-grain rice
¾ cup (180 ml) fresh cream
3 Tbsp (45 ml/45 g) soft butter
4 extra-large free-range eggs
700 g fresh salmon or trout, pin-boned and skinned
2 x 400 g rolls readymade puff pastry, thawed
⅓ cup (80 ml) finely chopped fresh dill
⅓ cup (80 ml) finely chopped flat-leaf parsley
1 tsp (5 ml) cayenne pepper, or more, to taste
zest and juice of 1 large lemon
salt and milled black pepper
1 beaten egg, for brushing

FOR THE SAUCE
juice of 1 large lemon
4 Tbsp (60 ml) capers, drained
1 cup (250 ml/250 g) melted butter

Boil the rice in 450 ml salted water for 15 minutes, or until just tender. Drain and return to the pot. Fluff it with a fork, stir in the cream and butter, cover and set aside. Boil the eggs in briskly simmering water for exactly 9 minutes. Plunge into cold water and set under a trickling tap for 3 minutes, or until completely cool. Put the salmon in a bowl and cover it with boiling water. Allow to stand for 3 minutes (it will still be raw on the inside). Drain the fish, then pull it into large flakes.

Heat the oven to 190 °C. Place a large sheet of baking paper on the counter and lightly flour it. Roll out the pastry to increase its size by about 2 cm on all sides. Trim the edges so you have a neat rectangle. Repeat with the second roll of pastry.

Stir the dill, parsley, cayenne pepper, lemon zest and juice into the cooled rice. Season generously with salt and pepper. Prick one of the pastry sheets all over with a fork. Spread three-quarters of the rice mixture on top, leaving a gap of 2 cm all round. Peel the eggs, cut into sixths lengthways and arrange on top of the rice. Scatter the salmon in between the eggs. Pat the remaining rice on top, filling in any gaps. Sprinkle with extra lemon juice, parsley and dill.

Paint the pastry edges with beaten egg. Lift the second sheet and place it on top of the first. Seal firmly by tucking the edges of the top sheet under the bottom one. Brush the pie with beaten egg and poke a few 5-mm slits in the top. Pick up the edges of the paper and slide the pie onto a baking sheet. Bake for 25–30 minutes, or until the pastry is puffed, golden and crisp.

Stir the lemon juice and capers into the melted butter. Serve the pie piping hot, with lemon wedges and fresh dill, and pass the sauce around in a small jug.

Serves 8.

Notes

This pie is spectacular served in the shape of a fish. Cut the pastry sheets into two identical fish-shapes, but ones with rather broad tails so there's plenty of space for the filling. Seal the edges and make a decorative border with the tines of a fork. Make a big eye and mouth using pastry trimmings, and use the rim of a wineglass to mark fish scales. The pie can be assembled 4–5 hours ahead of baking, but make sure the filling is completely cold before you spread it on the pastry.

Baked Fish with Walnut Tarator and Greek-Salad Salsa

Tarator is the name given to a family of sauces popular in Eastern Europe and across the Levant and Middle East. Some are yoghurty sauces similar to tzatziki, others contain bread, pine nuts, tahini, almonds or hazelnuts. This is a Turkish-style tarator which, despite containing strong-tasting walnuts, is surprisingly subtle, with an agreeable creamy texture.

2 kg linefish (see Notes)
olive oil and lemon juice for drizzling

FOR THE TARATOR
100 g shelled raw walnuts
2 fat cloves garlic, peeled and chopped
½ tsp (2.5 ml) salt
2 slices white bread
about ¾ cup (180 ml) warm water
juice of 1 lemon
100 ml olive oil
½ tsp (2.5 ml) ground cumin
1½ tsp (7.5 ml) paprika

FOR THE SALSA
½ English cucumber, halved and deseeded
½ onion, peeled and very finely chopped
1 Tbsp (15 ml) white wine vinegar
3 tomatoes, peeled and deseeded (see Notes)
12 calamata olives, pitted
80 g feta cheese
3 Tbsp (45 ml) olive oil
3 Tbsp (45 ml) chopped flat-leaf parsley
a pinch of dried red chilli flakes (optional)
salt and milled black pepper

Heat the oven to 200 °C.

First make the tarator. Put the walnuts, garlic and salt into a food processor (or use a mortar and pestle) and grind to a fine powder. Add the bread and just enough warm water to create a smooth, thick paste: start with ½ cup (125 ml), and then add more as required. Whizz in the lemon juice, a little at a time, until it's sharp enough for your liking. Now add the olive oil in a steady stream to create a thick, creamy sauce. Stir in the cumin and paprika. Chill.

To make the salsa, thinly slice the cucumber, sprinkle with a little salt and leave to drain in a colander for 20 minutes. Put the onion in a bowl and add the vinegar. Cut the tomatoes, olives and feta into a fine, even dice, trying to get every piece the same size. Pat the cucumber slices dry on kitchen paper, and dice. Put all the chopped ingredients into the bowl containing the onion and add the olive oil, parsley and chilli flakes, if you're using them. Season with salt and pepper, cover and chill.

Skin the fish and cut into eight neat steaks or fillets. Put the fish fillets on a baking sheet, drizzle with olive oil and lemon juice and bake for 10–15 minutes (see Notes). Slide each fillet onto a warm plate and top generously with the tarator. Arrange the salsa in a strip down the middle of each piece of fish. Serve immediately, with lemon wedges and a green salad.

Serves 8.

Notes

A meaty, firm-textured fish such as dorado or yellowtail is ideal for this dish, but you can use any sustainable white fish. How long the fish fillets will take to cook depends on their thickness (see Notes, p. 100). Prepare the tarator up to 2 days ahead (it improves after 24 hours in the fridge), but you may need to thin it with a little warm water before serving, as it thickens on standing. To peel tomatoes, cut a shallow cross in the top of each one. Put them in a bowl and cover with boiling water. Leave them for a minute or two, or until you see the skin begin to peel back where you made a cross. Lift the tomatoes from the water with a slotted spoon and slip off the skins.

Crumbed Baked Linefish with Whipped Caper Butter

A crunchy herb topping and swirls of creamy chilled butter make this easy dish a real crowd-pleaser. If you're not keen on capers, add your choice of interesting flavouring to the whipped butter: wholegrain mustard, mashed anchovies, lemon zest, chilli flakes, and so on.

2 kg white linefish, skinned and cut into 8 neat steaks or fillets

2 large day-old bread rolls, or enough to make 2½ cups (625 ml) crumbs

finely grated zest of 1 lemon

4 Tbsp (60 ml) chopped fresh herbs of your choice

150 ml finely grated Parmesan

salt and milled black pepper

3 Tbsp (45 ml) olive oil

150 g softened butter

3 Tbsp (45 ml) crème fraîche or thick sour cream

4 tsp (20 ml) capers, drained and finely chopped

1 Tbsp (15 ml) Dijon mustard

Pat the fish portions dry, remove any bones and arrange on a baking sheet lined with a sheet of baking paper. Put the bread rolls (in chunks) and lemon zest into a food processor and whizz to a fairly fine crumb. Add the herbs and pulse a few times until finely chopped (but don't over-process, or you'll end up with green dust). Tip the crumbs onto a large plate and mix in the Parmesan. Season with salt and pepper (but go easy on the salt as the Parmesan is quite salty). If you have time, put the plate, uncovered, in the fridge for a few hours so the crumbs can dry out a little. Sprinkle the olive oil over the crumb mixture and lightly rub it in, using your fingertips. Rub a film of oil over the top of the fish pieces and season with salt and pepper. Divide the mixture into eight and cover each piece of fish with a generous layer of crumbs, patting down lightly with the back of a spoon. Chill, uncovered, in the fridge for up to 6 hours.

Place the butter and crème fraîche in a bowl and beat with an electric whisk for 5 minutes, until light and fluffy. Mix in the capers and mustard and season with pepper, and more salt if required. Put the mixture into a piping bag fitted with a large nozzle and pipe eight big blobs onto a sheet of baking paper (if you don't have a piping bag, make dollops using a big spoon). Chill until needed.

Heat the oven to 200 °C. Bake the fish for 10–15 minutes, or until the fish is just cooked through and the crust is crisp. Put a blob of chilled butter on each portion and take straight to the table. Serve with lemon wedges, mashed potato and peas, or a green salad.

Serves 8.

Notes

How long the fish pieces will take to cook depends on their thickness and your oven (this works best with a fan-assisted oven, which helps to crisp up the crumb topping during a short cooking time). Test the fish for doneness after 10 minutes by cutting a slit in the thickest part of one of the fillets. You can assemble the crumbed fish stacks up to 6 hours ahead and keep them uncovered, on a plate lined with baking paper, in the fridge; the whipped butter can be made up to three days ahead.

Salmon, Dill and Potato Bake

It's very difficult to estimate how much liquid will be absorbed by the potatoes in a Dauphinoise-style dish like this, because no two batches of spud are alike. My solution is to partly cook the potatoes in milk and cream in advance, a method that allows you to judge the right amount of liquid, and this also helps to prevent the milk from curdling during baking. A comforting dish that makes a little fresh salmon go a long way.

350 ml fresh cream
about 2½ cups (625 ml) milk
½ onion, peeled and studded with
2 whole cloves
2 bay leaves
salt and milled black pepper
1.8 kg all-purpose potatoes
3 Tbsp (45 ml) butter, plus more for topping
600 g salmon or trout, pin-boned and skinned
2 tsp (10 ml) finely grated lemon zest
½ cup (125 ml) finely chopped fresh dill
1 clove garlic, peeled

Heat the oven to 170 °C.

Pour the cream and 2 cups (500 ml) of the milk into a large pan. Add the onion, the bay leaves and a pinch of salt and bring very slowly to the boil. As soon as the milk rises in the pot, turn off the heat and cover the surface with a sheet of clingfilm. Allow to stand for 5 minutes.

Using a mandolin or the slicing attachment on your food processor, cut the potatoes, crossways, into very thin slices. Tip the slices into the hot milk (and do so right away, or the potatoes will oxidise and turn brown) and add the butter. The slices will poke up above the surface of the milk. Turn the heat on under the pan and bring up to a simmer. After 5 minutes, gently press down on the slices using the back of a spatula, and then top up with just enough extra milk to barely cover the slices. Simmer for 6–7 minutes, or until the slices are just becoming tender, but still retain a slight bite. Season with pepper and more salt, if necessary.

Cut the salmon into 2-cm pieces and place in a bowl. Season lightly with salt and pepper, sprinkle with the lemon zest and dill and toss to coat. Cut the garlic clove in half lengthways and rub the cut sides over the base and sides of a large, shallow baking dish. Generously butter the dish. Using a slotted spoon, lift half the potatoes from the milk and spread them gently on the base of the dish (discard the onion and bay leaves). Arrange the salmon pieces on top, then top with the remaining potato slices. Press down lightly with the back of a spatula. Now add just enough of the hot milk/cream mixture to the potatoes until barely covered. They shouldn't be swimming in liquid, nor too dry. Scatter with a few pieces of butter and bake, uncovered, for 20–30 minutes, or until golden on top. Serve with a plain green salad.

Serves 8.

Notes

This dish should be assembled no longer than an hour before it goes into the oven, but you can partly cook the potatoes and coat the salmon pieces ahead of time, and keep them covered until you need them. This is also good with lightly smoked trout.

Mediterranean Tuna, Tomato and Potato Stew

I'm willing to bet that the only way you've eaten fresh tuna in the last few years is as sushi or in the form of fashionably raw seared steaks. Here's another way to serve this splendid fish, in a humble but most delicious one-pot Spanish dish based on a Marmitako, a traditional fish dish made by Basque fishermen. This is the ideal make-ahead dish for a feast, because the tuna is briefly poached at the very last minute.

750 g fresh tuna (see Notes)
4 Tbsp (60 ml) olive oil
2 red peppers, thinly sliced
2 large onions, peeled and finely chopped
2 green peppers, thinly sliced
1 x 20-cm stalk celery, thinly sliced
5 large cloves garlic, peeled and finely grated
2 Tbsp (30 ml) tomato paste
2 kg ripe red tomatoes, peeled (p. 99) and chopped
2 bay leaves
1 tsp (5 ml) dried red chilli flakes (optional)
2 tsp (10 ml) paprika
1½ cups (375 ml) dry white wine
1 x 10-cm strip of orange peel, white pith removed
1.2 kg potatoes, peeled and cut into big chunks
hot water (or fish stock, if you have it)
salt and milled black pepper
juice of ½ lemon
⅓ cup (80 ml) finely chopped fennel fronds or flat-leaf parsley

Trim the tuna and cut it into large (3–4 cm) cubes. Cover and set aside. Heat the olive oil over a high heat in a large, deep pan. When the oil is very hot (it should be shimmering, but not smoking) throw in the red pepper slices and cook, tossing, for a minute or two, until they just begin to scorch at the edges. Turn the heat down a little, add the onions, green peppers and celery, and fry over a medium heat for 3–4 minutes, or until the onions are soft. Stir in the garlic and tomato paste and cook for another minute. Add the chopped tomatoes, bay leaves, chilli flakes and paprika, turn down the heat and simmer briskly, stirring occasionally, for 12–15 minutes, or until the sauce has thickened slightly. Add the wine, orange peel and potato chunks. Now pour in just enough water or stock to completely cover the potato pieces. Season generously with salt and pepper. Cook, uncovered, at a lively simmer for 20–30 minutes, or until the potatoes are cooked right through, but nowhere near collapsing. Top up the sauce with more hot water as it reduces so the potatoes stay just covered. Cover and set aside until needed (see Notes).

Ten minutes before you're ready to serve it, bring the stew quickly back up to the boil, then turn the heat right down so it's barely simmering. Squeeze the lemon juice over the tuna chunks, season with a little salt and add to the stew, pushing them right down so the chunks are submerged. Simmer for exactly 3 minutes, gently shaking the pan now and then. Cut into one of the tuna pieces to check for doneness: if there's any sign of pinkness on the inside, simmer for another 1–2 minutes, or until the fish is just cooked through. Scatter over the chopped fennel leaves and take the dish straight to the table, in its pan. Serve with a green salad and buttered baguette slices for dipping.

Serves 8.

Notes

Use a sustainable tuna, namely pole-caught albacore or yellowfin tuna. This stew can be made up to 24 hours in advance, and reheated just before the fish is added. Pay great attention to timing when you add the fish to the pan: just one or two minutes too long, and the tuna will toughen and dry out, so set a timer to remind yourself. If you're on a tight budget, use tinned tuna in this dish, and cook it only long enough to warm it through.

Four-Pepper Prawns with Coconut and Cashew Rice

Butter-drenched prawns are among southern Africa's most adored celebratory dishes, and they usually involve chillies of some sort. Peppercorns tend to be overlooked as a heating agent, and this is a pity, because they have a special warmth and fragrance that really brings out the sweetness of prawns. With a meek-flavoured coconut and cashew rice as an accompaniment, this recipe is perfect for a very special feast.

1.5 kg prawns, heads on, deveined
4 large cloves garlic, peeled
1 tsp (5 ml) flaky sea salt
5 tsp (25 ml) brined green peppercorns, drained
4 tsp (20 ml) mixed dried white, black and pink peppercorns (see Notes)
4 Tbsp (60 ml) olive oil, plus extra for frying
finely grated zest and juice of 2 lemons
1 tsp (5 ml) dried red chilli flakes (optional)
2 tsp (10 ml) paprika
3 Tbsp (45 ml/45 g) butter

FOR THE RICE
500 g plain or Jasmine rice
1 x 400 ml tin coconut milk
a thumb-length strip of lemon peel, white pith removed
1 tsp (5 ml) salt
1 cup (250 ml) roasted, salted cashew nuts
⅓ cup (80 ml) finely chopped flat-leaf parsley

Pat the prawns dry and place them in a large bowl. Using a mortar and pestle or mini food processor, grind the garlic, salt, and all four types of peppercorn to a slightly coarse, gritty paste. Stir in the olive oil, lemon zest, chilli flakes and paprika. Tip the paste over the prawns and use your hands to mix everything together. Cover the bowl and put the prawns in the fridge for 1 hour, or longer (see Notes).

In the meantime, make the coconut rice. Put the rice into a pot and add the coconut milk, lemon peel and salt. Now add enough water to cover the rice to a depth of about 2 cm. Bring quickly to the boil, cover with a tilted lid, then turn down the heat and simmer briskly, without stirring, for 15 minutes, or until the rice is tender and almost all the liquid has evaporated. Drain in a colander, return the rice to the pot and cover tightly with a lid until needed.

Heat 2 Tbsp (30 ml) olive oil in a very large, shallow pan. When the oil is hot and shimmering, fry the prawns in two or three batches for 4–5 minutes, depending on their size, tossing the pan frequently. Put the cooked prawns on a plate while you fry the rest. Return all the prawns to the pan, turn down the heat to medium and add the butter. When the butter has melted, stir in the lemon juice and bubble for a further 2 minutes. Check the seasoning.

Gently reheat the rice, stir in the cashew nuts and season with more salt, if necessary. Tip the prawns and rice onto a heated platter, sprinkle with parsley, and take immediately to the table with a plate of lemon wedges.

Serves 8.

Notes

If you can find springy fresh prawns, or top-quality frozen ones from Mozambique, this is a dish worth splashing out on. (However, as prawns are orange-listed on the SASSI database this is a dish that should be reserved for very special occasions.) The prawns need to be cooked just before they're served, but you can make the peppercorn paste and the rice up to 6 hours in advance, and marinate the prawns up to 2 hours ahead. Mixed peppercorns are sold as 'rainbow peppercorns' and are available at supermarkets.

Chicken

Nothing epitomises a home feast like a plump golden chicken, cooked to perfection, served with rustling roast potatoes and jugfuls of gorgeous gravy. There's something about the succulence and aroma of a crisp-skinned roast chicken, or a creamy chicken pie, that evokes the happiest feelings in many people, no doubt because these are dishes fragrant with memories of Mum, home and childhood.

You won't find a recipe for plain roast chicken in this chapter, but there are interesting new dishes and some variations on old ones. All are designed to bring smiles to the faces of your friends and families and to deliver maximum flavour, comfort and joy.

Chicken may be a humble bird, but it's not easy to cook properly. The problem with chickens is that their tender breasts take less time to cook than their dense, succulent legs. By the time you've cooked the darker meat through to the bone, the breasts are often dry and stringy, and this is the ruin of many a good roast chicken. I solve this in various ways in this book: by basting them, marinating them, pulling the breasts away from the chicken before they've finished cooking in stock, and by putting some insulating stuffing or fat between breast and skin. Skinned boned breasts, so popular for their light, lean flesh, are particularly tricky because they turn into rubbery curls if you cook them too fiercely, or become unpleasantly stiff and chalky if left in the pan for too long. I always poach chicken breasts in the oven (p. 123) because I reckon this is the only foolproof way to achieve a juicy, tender breast without a hint of stringiness.

Do choose a good free-range chicken. Properly reared chickens are fat and firm, with a golden skin, and they always look fairly symmetrical. A lopsided, thin or flabby chicken with a blueish tinge should be avoided, as should frozen chicken pieces. You can save a lot of money by buying good big chickens and jointing or spatchcocking them yourself, and by buying whole breasts and removing the skin and bone with a few flicks of a sharp knife. This is a lot easier than it sounds: if you're not feeling confident, have a look at the excellent videos on the Internet.

Take care choosing the right quantities and suitable joints for each dish. A whole chicken, even a very large one, feeds only four people. Children don't much like thighs and wings, but they love drumsticks and breasts. Finally, the skin of chicken pieces should be browned to a golden crunch (though there are occasional exceptions). It's the sticky golden residue that chicken skin leaves on the bottom of a pan that holds the key to really deep and beautiful flavours.

Butterflied Chicken Stuffed with Ricotta and Artichokes

The idea for this recipe came about while I was scratching my head wondering what to do with the leftover dip on p. 14. It took a few tries to get the formula right, but I'm now besotted with this delicate, crumbly stuffing of ricotta cheese, artichoke hearts and lemon thyme. Pushed deep between the skin and the flesh, it keeps the chicken beautifully tender and juicy as it bakes. A lovely light summer dish, and very easy to make.

2 large free-range chickens, butterflied
2 cups (500 ml; about 400 g) fresh ricotta cheese
1 x 400 g tin artichoke hearts, drained and chopped
4 Tbsp (60 ml/60 g) soft butter
4 Tbsp (60 ml) finely grated Parmesan
3 Tbsp (45 ml) fresh white breadcrumbs
2 cloves garlic, peeled and crushed
2 sprigs of lemon thyme, leaves stripped (see Notes)
salt and milled black pepper
1 large onion, peeled and thinly sliced
1 large carrot, peeled and thinly sliced
juice of 1 large lemon
½ cup (125 ml) water, white wine or stock, or a mixture

Heat the oven to 180 °C.

Push your fingertips, gently but firmly, under the skin over the breasts to form a pocket (use a hooked finger to pull at the membrane joining them). Now poke your fingertips deep into the skin over the thighs and the thick ends of the drumsticks, gently pushing and probing until all the skin is loosened.

Mix together the ricotta, artichokes, butter, Parmesan, breadcrumbs, garlic and thyme leaves and season with a little salt and pepper. Push the mixture under the skin of the chickens, stuffing a little filling right down into the thighs and drumsticks and spreading the rest over the breasts. Pat and smooth the skin so the stuffing is evenly distributed over the breasts and the whole chicken looks nice and plump. If the skin has crept back from the thinner ends of the breasts, pull it back into place and secure it with a few toothpicks.

Arrange the sliced onion and carrot in two piles in a large roasting pan. Place the chickens on top of the vegetables, squeeze the lemon juice over them and season with salt and pepper. Roast for 55–65 minutes, basting the chickens now and then with the pan juices, until cooked right through. Take the chickens out of the pan and set aside on a plate to rest for 5–10 minutes.

Set the pan over a medium heat and pour in the water, wine or stock, stirring briskly to dislodge any sediment. Pour the juices that have accumulated under the chickens into the pan and bubble for a few minutes. Season with salt and pepper. Put the chickens on a large, warmed platter and strain the pan juices over them. Serve with baked potatoes or a potato salad, and some green leaves, such as rocket or watercress, dressed with olive oil and lemon juice.

Serves 8.

Notes

If you can't find lemon thyme, use ordinary fresh thyme and add the finely grated zest of a lemon. The birds can be stuffed and kept covered in the fridge, ready for baking, up to 8 hours ahead.

Spiced Butterflied Chicken with Saffron and Yoghurt

This is an easy oven-baked dish that adds great flavour and succulence to whole chickens. It doesn't take long to prepare, but it does need to marinate in its spicy, yoghurty cloak for two to three hours.

2 large free-range chickens, butterflied
1 thin slice of lemon, peel on
3 bay leaves
2 sprigs of fresh thyme
1½ cups (375 ml) thick natural yoghurt
3 cloves garlic, peeled and finely grated
3 Tbsp (45 ml) grated fresh ginger
juice of 2 lemons
1 Tbsp (15 ml) tomato paste
1 tsp (5 ml) chilli powder (or more, to taste, and optional)
2 tsp (10 ml) ground cumin
2 tsp (10 ml) garam masala
2 tsp (10 ml) ground coriander
1 tsp (5 ml) ground cinnamon
a pinch of saffron threads (or 1½ tsp (7.5 ml) turmeric)
salt and milled black pepper
a little melted butter, for basting
a small bunch of fresh coriander
lemon wedges

Using a sharp knife, make deep diagonal slashes in the thighs, breasts and drumsticks of the chickens. Put the lemon slice, bay leaves and fresh thyme sprigs in a large roasting pan and lay the chickens, skin-side up, on top. In a bowl, whisk together the yoghurt, garlic, ginger, lemon juice, tomato paste and all the spices. Season with salt and pepper.

Pour the mixture over the chickens and rub into the skin, pressing it deeply into the cuts. For even more flavour, gently separate the breast skin from the meat and spread some of the marinade into the pocket you've made. Cover the pan with clingfilm and marinate in the fridge for 2–3 hours (and no more than 4 hours).

Heat the oven to 180 °C. Grind a little salt and pepper over the top of the chickens and bake for 55–65 minutes, or until cooked through (p. 123). Baste the chickens two or three times with the pan juices and a little melted butter as they're roasting.

Take the chickens out of the pan and set aside to rest for 5–10 minutes. Cut into portions, scatter with some freshly chopped coriander and serve hot, with lemon wedges. This is good with boiled new potatoes and a simple salad of dark leaves dressed with the strained hot pan juices.

Serves 8.

Notes

Go easy on the saffron – see Notes on p. 112. Don't be tempted to add more than one slice of lemon to the roasting pan, or it will make the juices bitter.

Chicken à la Bourride

In this sunny soul-cheerer of a dish, I've cooked chicken in the style of bourride, a traditional Provençal seafood stew thickened with garlicky homemade aïoli. I make this with meaty bone-in chicken breasts because everyone seems to like them, but you can use thighs or a mixture of chicken joints. If there are children at the table, set aside some of the tomato sauce before you add the fennel and orange peel.

8 large free-range chicken breasts, on the bone
salt and milled black pepper
3 Tbsp (45 ml) sunflower or olive oil
2 large onions, peeled and finely chopped
3 carrots, peeled and diced
6 large, ripe tomatoes, peeled (p. 99) and coarsely chopped
3 cloves garlic, peeled and finely chopped
1 cup (250 ml) dry white wine
1 cup (250 ml) Chicken Stock (p. 187) or water
2 Tbsp (30 ml) tomato paste
2 large sprigs of fresh thyme
1 bay leaf
1 tsp (5 ml) fennel seeds, coarsely ground
2 strips orange peel as long as your thumb, white pith removed
a pinch of saffron threads (optional)
4 Tbsp (60 ml) finely chopped flat-leaf parsley

FOR THE AÏOLI
300 ml Mayonnaise (p. 186) made using olive oil and lemon juice
4 cloves garlic or more, to taste, peeled and crushed
2 tsp (10 ml) Dijon mustard

Season the chicken breasts with salt and pepper. Heat the oil in a large pan big enough to hold all the pieces in a single layer (see Notes, p. 116). Fry the breasts, skin-side down, and in two batches, over a medium-high heat for 3–4 minutes, or until the skin is golden and crisp. Set aside on a plate. Drain all but 2 Tbsp (30 ml) of the fat from the pan and turn the heat down to medium. Add the onions and carrots and cook for 4–5 minutes, or until the onions are soft and golden. Add the chopped tomatoes to the pan, along with the garlic. Turn up the heat again and cook at a brisk bubble for 8–10 minutes, or until slightly reduced and thickened. Add the wine, stock, tomato paste, thyme, bay leaf, fennel seeds, orange peel and saffron. Cook over a medium heat for 15 minutes, stirring occasionally. Return the chicken pieces, skin-side up, to the pan; the skins should poke up out of the liquid. Cover and simmer gently for 30 minutes, or until the chicken is cooked right through, shaking the pan occasionally.

To make the aïoli, mix the mayonnaise with the crushed garlic and mustard. Cover and chill.

Using a pair of tongs, remove the chicken pieces from the pan and set aside. Cool the sauce for 5 minutes or so; it should be hot but not scalding. Put ½ cup (125 ml) of the aïoli in a small bowl. Add two ladles of sauce to the aïoli to temper it, whisk until smooth, then pour the mixture back into the pan and stir well. Return the chicken pieces and any accumulated juices to the pan and cook for a few minutes over a very low heat, gently shaking the pan so the sauce thickens evenly. Don't allow the sauce to boil furiously, or it may curdle. Scatter over the parsley and serve hot, passing around the remaining aïoli in a separate bowl. This is excellent with crusty bread and a light leafy salad, or with mashed potatoes or rice.

Serves 8.

Notes

You can make this in advance and keep it covered in the fridge, but the sauce must be warmed and thickened with the aïoli just before you serve the dish. Take care not to overcook the breasts, which will make them dry and stringy. Use just a small pinch of saffron (8–10 threads): it's a powerful spice and too much of it will overwhelm the other flavours.

Luxurious Chicken Pie with Bacon and Sage Stuffing Balls

Nuggets of stuffing flavoured with bacon, lemon and sage add an interesting twist to this comforting and creamy pie. This dish takes time to make, and has a lot of ingredients, but both are necessary to create a sumptuous pie with a deep, satisfying flavour.

1 x 400 g roll readymade puff pastry
1 extra-large free-range egg,
lightly beaten

FOR THE FILLING
2 free-range chickens
salt and milled black pepper
1 stalk celery, sliced
2 bay leaves
1 onion, studded with 3 whole cloves
1 large sprig of thyme
1 lemon
2 cloves garlic, peeled
4 cups (1 litre) water
1½ cups (375 ml) white wine

FOR THE STUFFING
1 onion, peeled and very finely chopped
5 rashers streaky or back bacon, diced
2 Tbsp (30 ml) olive oil
finely grated zest of 1 small lemon
4 fresh sage leaves, finely chopped
3 large slices day-old white bread
1 extra-large free-range egg, lightly beaten
sunflower oil for frying

FOR THE BÉCHAMEL SAUCE
6 Tbsp (90 ml/90 g) butter
100 ml cake flour
1½ cups (375 ml) milk
¼ tsp (1.25 ml) grated nutmeg
2 tsp (10 ml) Dijon mustard
4 tsp (20 ml) brandy
5 Tbsp (75 ml) fresh cream
4 Tbsp (60 ml) chopped fresh parsley
a little lemon juice
salt and milled black pepper

Heat the oven to 180 °C. For the filling, place the chickens in a deep roasting pan, season with salt and pepper inside and out and add the celery, bay leaves, onion and thyme. Squeeze the lemon over the chickens, then put the squeezed-out halves and the garlic cloves into the cavity. Tie the ends of the drumsticks together with string. Pour the water and wine into the pan and roast for 1 hour and 20 minutes, or until the chickens are cooked through (p. 123). Tip any juice from the cavity of the chickens back into the pan and set the chickens aside on a plate to cool for a while. Strip off the flesh and tear it into large strips. Put the skin and bones back into the roasting pan, place over a moderate heat and simmer for 40 minutes. Strain the stock into a jug, cool and skim off any fat. Measure out 2 cups (500 ml).

For the stuffing, fry the onion and bacon in the oil for 3–4 minutes, or until the onion is soft and golden and the bacon is beginning to crisp. Stir in the lemon zest and sage. Tear up the bread and whizz to fine crumbs. Place the crumbs in a bowl, add the onion mixture and beaten egg and mix lightly together. Form the mixture into balls the size of large marbles and fry over a medium heat in a little oil until golden brown on all sides. Set aside.

Make a béchamel sauce (p. 188) using the butter, flour and milk. Remove from the heat and stir in the reserved stock, nutmeg, mustard, brandy, cream, parsley and a spritz of lemon juice. Season with salt and pepper. When the sauce has cooled, mix it with the chicken strips. Tip the filling into a large greased pie dish (or individual dishes) and arrange the stuffing balls on top. Lightly roll out the pastry so it's about 2 cm bigger on all sides, and trim to the size and shape of your pie dish. Drape the pastry over the dish and seal the edges by lightly pressing and crimping them. Brush with beaten egg and use any pastry trimmings to make leafy decorations. Cut a 1-cm slit in the middle of the pastry. Bake for 30–40 minutes, or until the pastry is crisp and golden and the filling is bubbling.

Serves 8.

Notes	This filling can be made a day ahead, and the pie assembled up to 8 hours in advance, but make sure that the filling is quite cold when you put it into the pie dish. Use a good-quality butter puff pastry.

Chicken with Cider, Bacon and Mushrooms

This creamy, comforting crowd-pleaser is a coq-au-vin-style dish, but made with dry cider, which has a great affinity with chicken. If you can find fresh tarragon, use it by all means, but I find that good-quality dried tarragon is just as pungent. If there are children at the table, you might want to leave the mushrooms out of a portion of the dish.

2 free-range chickens or a selection of chicken pieces of your choice
3 Tbsp (45 ml/45 g) butter
1 Tbsp (15 ml) olive oil
3 large leeks, rinsed and finely sliced
250 g back bacon, diced
3 cloves garlic, peeled and finely chopped
500 g tiny button mushrooms
3 cups (750 ml) dry cider
2½ tsp (12.5 ml) dried tarragon
1 big sprig of thyme
salt and milled black pepper
1½ cups (375 ml) fresh cream
4 Tbsp (60 ml) finely chopped curly parsley

Remove any visible fat from the chickens and cut them into 16 portions (or ask your butcher to do this for you). Heat the butter and olive oil in a large, shallow pan, add the leeks and bacon and fry gently over a medium heat for 4–5 minutes, without allowing the leeks to brown. Add the garlic and cook for another minute. Remove the leeks, bacon and garlic using a slotted spoon and set aside, leaving no traces that could blacken during the next step.

Brown the chicken pieces on both sides, over a high heat and in batches, for 3–4 minutes, or until the skin is crisp and golden (add a little more butter or oil to the pan if necessary). Set aside on a plate. Drain off all but 1 Tbsp (15 ml) of the fat, add the mushrooms and fry over a high heat for 2–3 minutes, or until they begin to turn golden. Pour in the cider and bubble briskly for 3 minutes, stirring and scraping to dislodge the golden sediment on the bottom of the pan. Return the chicken (skin-side up), leeks, garlic and bacon to the pan and add the tarragon, thyme sprig and a big pinch of salt. Reduce the heat and bubble, uncovered, for 25–30 minutes, or until the chicken is cooked right through. Turn the chicken pieces over three or four times while they cook. Remove the thyme sprig, stir in the cream, season to taste with salt and pepper and cook gently for a few more minutes, or until the sauce has reduced slightly and thickened. Scatter with parsley and serve hot with mashed or crushed potatoes and a green salad or vegetables.

Serves 8.

Notes

You'll need to make this in a large shallow pan because the cider won't reduce properly in a pot with a small surface area. An electric frying pan is ideal. If you don't have a pan big enough, use two big frying pans. You can make this a few hours in advance, but add the cream and the parsley just before you serve it.

Coronation Chicken with New Potatoes

You don't often see Coronation Chicken on menus or in books these days, but I'm a fervent fan of this splendid classic of the Fifties. In my lighter, brighter version, I've included a number of spices to give the dish a more complex, layered taste, and combined the chicken with baby potatoes to create a substantial cold one-dish summer meal.

2 large free-range chickens
salt and milled black pepper
1 lemon
1 onion, peeled and halved
2 bay leaves
2 cloves garlic, peeled and lightly crushed
1.5 kg new potatoes

FOR THE SAUCE
3 Tbsp (45 ml) sunflower oil
2 tsp (10 ml) black mustard seeds
1 stick of cinnamon
3 cardamom pods, lightly crushed
1 large onion, peeled and cut to a very fine dice
2 cloves garlic, peeled and finely grated
a thumb-sized piece fresh ginger, finely grated
1 bay leaf
2 thin slices of lemon, peel on
4 tsp (20 ml) tomato paste
5 Tbsp (75 ml) white wine
3 Tbsp (45 ml) apricot jam or chutney
1 tsp (5 ml) ground cumin
1 tsp (5 ml) turmeric
1 Tbsp (15 ml) medium-strength curry powder
1 cup (250 ml) Mayonnaise (p. 186) or Hellmann's original
¾ cup (180 ml) thick natural yoghurt
½ cup (125 ml) sour cream
juice of 1 lemon
½ cup (125 ml) finely chopped parsley
a little cayenne pepper

Heat the oven to 180 °C. Put the chickens into a deep roasting pan and season inside and out with salt and pepper. Sprinkle with lemon juice and push the squeezed-out halves into the cavities with the onion halves, bay leaves and garlic. Tie the ends of the drumsticks together with string. Pour water into the roasting pan to a depth of 3 cm. Cover tightly with foil and bake for 1 hour and 20 minutes, or until the chicken is cooked through. Set aside, still covered, to cool.

In the meantime, cover the potatoes with cold salted water, bring to the boil and cook for 15–20 minutes, or until just tender. Drain in a colander.

To make the sauce, heat the oil in a frying pan and add the mustard seeds, cinnamon stick and cardamom pods. Fry over a medium-high heat until the mustard seeds begin to crackle. Add the onion, garlic and ginger, turn down the heat and cook gently for 4 minutes, or until the onion is soft and translucent. Add the bay leaf, lemon slices, tomato paste, white wine, jam and 5 Tbsp (75 ml) of the liquid in which you cooked the chicken. Cook at a fairly brisk bubble for 7–8 minutes, or until the sauce has reduced to a somewhat thick, shiny glaze. Stir in the cumin, turmeric and curry powder and cook for another minute. Set aside to cool completely. Discard the cinnamon, bay leaves, lemon and cardamom.

Strip the chicken flesh from the bones and tear it into large flakes. Cut the potatoes in half crossways. Lightly whisk the mayonnaise, yoghurt and sour cream together in a large mixing bowl. Add the spicy sauce, a few tablespoons at a time, to the mayonnaise mixture until the dressing tastes right for you. I like it quite strong-flavoured, but you might prefer to keep it mild. Stir in the lemon juice, chicken strips and potatoes. Season generously with salt and pepper and toss gently to combine. Tip onto a large, deep platter and chill for 2 hours. Scatter with freshly chopped parsley and dust with a little cayenne pepper. Serve with a mixed green salad and some hot crisp poppadums.

Serves 8.

Notes | You can cook the chicken, make the sauce and boil the potatoes well in advance, then assemble at the last minute.

Moroccan-Spiced Chicken Pie

I'm smitten with the particular fragrance of North African spicing, and in this phyllo-topped pie I've used some of the flavours you might find in a chicken tagine. I'm not a great fan of cinnamon in savoury dishes, but there's something about the combination of this spice and preserved lemon that makes my tongue want to tie itself in happy knots.

12 skinless, deboned chicken breasts
5 sheets phyllo pastry
melted butter, for brushing
a little cinnamon and icing sugar, for dusting

FOR THE MARINADE
1 cup (250 ml) thick natural yoghurt
juice of 2 lemons
2 tsp (10 ml) finely grated lemon zest
2 cloves garlic, peeled and crushed
4 tsp (20 ml) ground cumin
1 tsp (5 ml) chilli powder (optional)

FOR THE SAUCE
2 Tbsp (30 ml) sunflower oil
2 onions, peeled and very finely chopped
1 stick of cinnamon
6 ripe, juicy tomatoes, peeled and quartered
6 Tbsp (90 ml) ground almonds
2 tsp (10 ml) ground ginger
2 tsp (10 ml) ground coriander
1 Tbsp (15 ml) mild paprika
2 cloves garlic, peeled and finely grated
1½ cups (375 ml) chicken stock or water
5 Tbsp (75 ml/75 g) cold butter, cubed
24 green olives, pitted
3 Tbsp (45 ml) finely chopped preserved lemon
½ cup (125 ml) chopped fresh coriander
½ cup (125 ml) chopped fresh parsley
salt and milled black pepper

Cut the chicken into strips as big as your pinkie finger (or into large cubes, if you prefer). Combine all the marinade ingredients in a large non-metallic bowl and stir in the chicken pieces. Cover and chill for an hour or two (but no longer than 4 hours).

To make the sauce, heat the oil in a large, shallow pan, add the onions and cinnamon stick and cook over a medium heat for 3–4 minutes, or until the onions are soft. Whizz the tomatoes to a pale pink, mushy liquid in a food processor. Pour this into the pan, stir in the almonds, ginger, ground coriander, paprika, garlic and stock and cook at a lively bubble for 10–15 minutes, or until the sauce has reduced and thickened slightly (draw a wooden spoon across the base of the pan: if the channel you've created closes with reluctance, the sauce is thick enough). Stir the chicken and its marinade into the pan and cook gently (the mixture should barely bubble) for 7–9 minutes, or until the chicken is just cooked through but still very tender. Stir in the cold butter, olives, preserved lemon, coriander and parsley. Season to taste with salt and pepper. Set aside to cool.

Heat the oven to 180 °C. Place a sheet of pastry on a piece of baking paper. Brush with melted butter, place another sheet on top and continue layering and brushing until you've used up all five sheets. Grease a pie dish that's a little smaller than the pastry. Pile the filling into the dish (discard the cinnamon) and place the phyllo stack on top. Tuck the overhanging pastry down along the edges, or crimp neatly. Brush melted butter over the pastry and dust with a little cinnamon and icing sugar. If you're making individual pies, find a saucer a little bigger than your pie dishes. Place it face-down on the layered pastry and cut around it with a knife. Place the circles on top of the pie dishes and tuck in the edges.

Bake for 20–30 minutes, or until the pastry is crisp and golden. If the pastry looks as if it's browning too quickly, cover loosely with foil. Serve immediately.

Serves 8.

Notes | This filling can be prepared the day before, and you can assemble the pie up to 3 hours before you bake it. Keep it tightly covered with clingfilm to prevent the pastry from drying out, and bring it up to room temperature before you bake it.

Poached Chicken with Lime and Lemongrass Cream Sauce

This delicate, silky sauce, enriched with cream and egg yolks and zinged with citrus, is lovely with tender poached chicken. This dish is my number one choice for a cooling lunch on a hot day.

10 skinless, deboned chicken breasts
1 small onion, peeled and thickly sliced
8 peppercorns
1 bay leaf
a few sprigs of parsley
1 slice of lemon, peel on
4 Tbsp (60 ml) dry white wine
a little lime or lemon juice
salt

FOR THE SAUCE
2 stalks lemongrass, lower parts only, bruised and sliced
1½ cups (375 ml) fresh cream
3 Tbsp (45 ml) butter
3 Tbsp (45 ml) cake flour
1 tsp (5 ml) finely grated lime or lemon zest
3 Tbsp (45 ml) lime or lemon juice
3 extra-large free-range egg yolks
½ tsp (2.5 ml) cornflour
salt and a pinch of white pepper

FOR GARNISHING
thin slices of lime
3 Tbsp (45 ml) finely snipped chives
⅓ cup (80 ml) toasted flaked almond

Heat the oven to 180 °C. Arrange the chicken in a single layer in an ovenproof dish and add the onion, peppercorns, bay leaf, parsley, lemon slice and wine. Pour over hot water to cover the breasts to a depth of 5 mm. Cook, uncovered, in the oven for 25–35 minutes, or until done (see Notes). Strain 450 ml of the cooking liquid into a jug and set aside. Drain the chicken and tear into big strips or flakes. Sprinkle with lime juice and season lightly with salt. Cover and refrigerate.

Place the lemongrass in a saucepan, add the cream and bring gently to the boil. Turn off the heat, cover and set aside for 1 hour. Strain the cream into a clean bowl. Set aside. Melt the butter in a saucepan, stir in the flour and cook for 1 minute. Whisk in the reserved 450 ml poaching liquid and bring to the boil, stirring constantly with a whisk as the sauce thickens. Cook gently for 2 minutes, remove from the heat and stir in the lime zest and 2 Tbsp (30 ml) of the lime juice.

Put the egg yolks and cornflour into the bowl containing the cooled cream and whisk for 30 seconds, until creamy. Stir a quarter of the hot sauce into the cream-egg yolk mixture to temper it, then strain this mixture back into the saucepan. Place the pan over a very low heat and cook gently, stirring all the time, for 3–4 minutes, or until very hot and thick enough to coat the back of a wooden spoon. Don't allow the sauce to get near boiling point, or it may curdle. Season with salt and white pepper and add a little more lime juice if you think the sauce needs sharpening. Cover the surface of the sauce with clingfilm and chill.

An hour or two before you're ready to serve, drain the chicken pieces, stir them into the sauce and return the pot to the fridge so the flavours can mingle. Arrange the chicken on a large platter and decorate with slices of lime, snipped chives and almond flakes. Serve with hot new potatoes and a leafy salad.

Serves 8.

Notes

The cornflour in this recipe helps to stabilise the sauce, but you can leave it out if you're confident about making egg-thickened sauces. The chicken may be poached up to 6 hours ahead and kept covered, in its liquid, in the fridge. How long the chicken breasts will take to cook to perfection depends on their size. Check for doneness after 25 minutes by cutting a slit in the thick part of one of the breasts; if there's any pinkness, cook for a few more minutes.

Bunny Chow with Butter Chicken

A hollowed-out half- or quarter-loaf of white bread brimming with a hot, highly spiced Durban-style curry is one of South Africa's most cherished street foods. In this, my not-at-all-authentic version, I've used a fragrant, sinfully rich filling based on a butter chicken formula. The spicing here is quite gentle, the way I like it, so add some fresh green chillies if you'd like to give the dish a bit of a kick.

12 skinless, deboned chicken breasts
3 cloves garlic, peeled and crushed
3 Tbsp (45 ml) finely grated fresh ginger
juice of 1 large lemon
1½ tsp (7.5 ml) chilli powder

FOR THE MARINADE
1½ cups (375 ml) thick natural yoghurt
1½ tsp (7.5 ml) garam masala
1 tsp (5 ml) ground cumin
1 tsp (5 ml) ground coriander
½ tsp (2.5 ml) turmeric
½ tsp (2.5 ml) salt
1 Tbsp (15 ml) sunflower oil

FOR THE SAUCE
1 kg ripe, juicy tomatoes, peeled (p. 99)
3 Tbsp (45 ml) tomato paste
1 tsp (5 ml) fenugreek seeds, coarsely crushed
1 stick of cinnamon
1 tsp (5 ml) ground cumin
1 tsp (5 ml) garam masala
½ tsp (2.5 ml) turmeric
salt and milled black pepper
1½ cups (375 ml) fresh cream
5 Tbsp (75 ml/75 g) cold butter

FOR SERVING
8 large crisp bread rolls
melted butter, for brushing

Cut three or four deep slashes in the chicken breasts and place in a bowl with the garlic, ginger, lemon juice and chilli powder. Rub the mixture into the chicken, pressing it well into the slashes, and set aside for 30 minutes. In a separate bowl, combine all the ingredients for the marinade. Pour this over the chicken breasts, mix well, cover and place in the fridge for 1–2 hours (but no longer than 3 hours).

Heat the oven to 200 °C. Lift the breasts from the bowl and, without wiping off the marinade, place in a single layer in an ovenproof dish. Bake for 7 minutes, turn down the heat to 170 °C and cook for a further 10–12 minutes, or until there is no trace of pinkness when you cut into the flesh of the chicken. Set aside.

To make the sauce, whizz the tomatoes to a coarse slush in a food processor and place in a large, shallow pan, adding the tomato paste, fenugreek, cinnamon, cumin, garam masala, turmeric and salt. Cook over a brisk heat for 8–12 minutes, or until the pulp has thickened slightly and reduced (when you pull a wooden spoon through the sauce, it should leave a gap that closes reluctantly). Stir in the cream, reduce the heat, and simmer for another 5 minutes.

Cut the tops off the rolls and hollow out the insides, leaving a 5 mm 'wall'. Brush the cut edges, lids and sides of the rolls with a little melted butter. Place the rolls and lids on a baking sheet and bake at 190 °C for 3–5 minutes, or until the edges are golden and crisp. Cut the chicken into bite-sized pieces, stir it into the sauce and cook over a very gentle heat for a few minutes, until the chicken pieces are heated right through. Cut the cold butter into cubes and stir them, one by one, into the sauce. Once all the butter has melted, season with pepper (and more salt, if necessary) and add a spritz of lemon juice to sharpen the sauce.

Pile the chicken into the warm rolls and top each one with a lid. Serve immediately.

Serves 8.

Notes

This dish can be prepared up to 6 hours ahead, but the cooked chicken pieces and butter should be added to the sauce at the last minute, and the rolls crisped while you're reheating the sauce.

Pot-Roasted Chicken with a Thousand Cloves of Garlic

Of course this recipe doesn't contain anywhere near a thousand cloves, but I think this is a fitting title for a dish of such extravagant garlickiness. This is the quickest-ever recipe to prepare for a feast, a wonderful, finger-licking dish that fills the house with delicious aromas as it cooks. To serve, plonk the pot in the middle of the table, chip off the paste to release fragrant clouds of steam and invite your guests to reach in ...

2 x 2 kg free-range chickens
salt and milled black pepper
5 whole heads of garlic
1½ cups (375 ml) dry white wine, such as a crisp Sauvignon Blanc
a small bunch of fresh herbs of your choice: rosemary, thyme, oregano, and so on
2 thin slices of lemon, peel on

FOR THE SEALING PASTE
1 cup (250 ml) cake flour
about ½ cup (125 ml) cold water

Set the oven to 180 °C. Season the chickens generously with salt and pepper, inside and out, and place them in a deep cast-iron lidded pot big enough to hold both (see Notes). Break the garlic into cloves and scatter them in the pot along with the wine and herbs. Tuck a few cloves, squashed with a heavy knife, and the lemon slices into the cavity of each chicken.

To make the sealing paste, mix the flour and water to a thick, wet, spreadable paste, adding a little more water if necessary. Don't overmix, or it will become stringy. Now 'glue' the lid to the pot by spreading a thick layer of paste all the way around the edges, smoothing it with your fingertip to form a tight seal. Don't worry about any mess: the paste will lift away easily once it's baked.

Bake the dish for 1¾ hours (105 minutes), without lifting the lid. Take the pot straight to the table and chip away the paste with a blunt knife. Provide your guests with plates and plenty of fresh, crusty bread, and invite them to dig straight into the pot, pulling the chickens to pieces, squeezing out the garlic pulp, and mopping up the juices with bread. This is good with Lemony Green Beans (p. 32) and Crisp Squashed Potatoes (p. 66).

Serves 8.

Notes

Don't worry if your pot isn't big enough to hold the chickens side by side: it's fine to let one rest on the other. If you don't have a lidded cast-iron pot, you can get away with a large deep roasting pan tightly covered with three layers of heavy foil, but don't be tempted to peek. I don't bother browning the chickens before they go into the pan, but if you'd like the chickens golden brown, fry them, top and bottom, in a mixture of olive oil and butter, before you add the remaining ingredients.

Meat

All but two of the recipes in this chapter require long, slow cooking, or can be prepared well in advance, or both. This is the way it should be, I think, when you're planning a meat course for an important feast.

The tempo of a festive meal is disrupted by a host who vanishes into the kitchen for long stretches before the main, meaty event. I don't think you should have to spend more than 10 or 12 minutes attending to last-minute details such as carving and gravy-making. If you think your dish is going to need more time than that, rope in one of your guests to help, and make sure that you've got all the platters, serving spoons, garnishes and other bits and pieces all lined up and ready to go.

Another advantage of slow-cooked dishes is that they are very forgiving, and can usually be placed on hold if there's any delay in the proceedings. A large roast, for example, can slumber happily beneath a layer of foil and a folded blanket for a good 40 minutes and suffer no harm, whereas a stir-fry or similar last-minute dish will lose all its vigour and vim if made to wait.

Also, slow cooking brings out the best in less expensive cuts of meat, and allows flavours to blossom over time. You can, of course, as TV chefs keep reminding us, produce a reasonably tasty meat course in under 30 minutes, but it is unlikely to have the deep, satisfying deliciousness or the mellow layers of flavour of a dish that's been patiently assembled well in advance by a calm and unhurried cook.

Finally, and most important, all this effort is wasted if you start out with a mediocre piece of meat. Buying any old joint from a supermarket is false economy; you will feel cheated when the end result doesn't seem worth the money you spent. Although some supermarkets have excellent in-house butchers, most meat sold in chain stores is unimpressive and (infuriatingly) they hardly ever seem to have exactly the piece of meat you're looking for. A far better approach is to visit a good butcher two or three days ahead of your feast, show him the recipe you're planning to make and order the meat there and then.

When I was a young cook, I was too shy to go into a butcher to ask for advice for fear of seeming an ignoramus, and it took many expensive failures before I realised that a really good piece of meat selected by a knowledgeable butcher makes all the difference to the end dish.

Lemony Lamb Shoulder with Potatoes en Papillote

For over fifteen years this heavenly dish of slow-cooked, fragrant, fall-apart lamb has been my favourite recipe for a feast. I used to serve it with roast potatoes but, as it's very rich, these days I pack tiny spuds in baking paper well ahead of time, sling them in the oven and bring the packets to the table all puffed and golden and painted with cheering messages (see Notes).

2 large shoulders of lamb, bone in, or
2 legs of lamb (see Notes)
12 fat cloves garlic, peeled
½ tsp (2.5 ml) flaky sea salt
finely grated zest of 2 lemons
3 Tbsp (45 ml) good-quality dried oregano
2 Tbsp (30 ml) olive oil
2 large onions, peeled and sliced
milled black pepper
1½ cups (375 ml) dry white wine, plus more for topping up
juice of 2 large lemons, plus more for topping up
2 bunches flat-leaf parsley

FOR THE POTATOES
2 kg tiny new potatoes
salt and milled black pepper
4 Tbsp (60 ml/60 g) butter
sprigs of fresh thyme
finely grated zest of 1 lemon
a little melted butter, for brushing

Heat the oven to 150 °C. Cut any large blobs of fat off the lamb. Finely grate six of the garlic cloves, place in a bowl and stir in the salt, lemon zest, 1 Tbsp (15 ml) of the oregano and the olive oil. Using a sharp knife, pierce the thick parts of the lamb (top and bottom) in 8–10 places, at a diagonal, to a depth of 3 cm. Push a little garlic paste deep into each cut and rub any remaining paste over the top of the joints. Put the onion slices and remaining garlic cloves into a large roasting pan and place the lamb on top. Sprinkle with the remaining oregano and plenty of black pepper, pour in the wine and lemon juice and cover tightly with two layers of heavy foil. Place in the oven. After 3½ hours, remove the foil, turn the heat down to 140 °C and switch off the oven fan. Season the lamb with salt, to taste. Roast, basting now and then with the pan juices, for a further 1½ hours, or until the lamb is brown and sticky and falling off the bone. Top up with more wine and lemon juice if necessary: the liquid in the pan should be about 1 cm deep.

For the potatoes, cut out eight circles of baking paper, each the size of a dinner plate. Prick the potatoes and divide them between the paper circles. Season with salt and pepper and add a knob of butter, a sprig of thyme, a sprinkling of lemon zest, and any other flavourings you fancy. Fold each circle in half to make a semicircle and tightly seal the edges by making small, overlapping pleats all the way round. Brush the tops of the parcels with melted butter and place on a baking sheet. An hour before you're ready to serve the lamb, place the parcels in the oven and bake for the remaining time or until quite tender (see Notes).

Lay a bed of flat-leaf parsley on a large platter and place the lamb on top. Cover with foil and allow to rest for 10 minutes. Pour the juices from the pan into a small jug and skim off the fat. Serve hot, with the potato parcels, and pass the pan juices round in a jug.

Serves 6 if you're using one shoulder; 12 if you use two.

Notes

A large bone-in lamb shoulder will feed six hungry people, but not eight, so I suggest you order two smaller shoulders, which will leave you with plenty of leftovers. If you have a second oven, you can bake the potatoes at 180 °C; they will take 30–40 minutes. Paint a message on each parcel using a fine paintbrush or calligraphy nib dipped in soy sauce.

Lamb Shank Curry with a Coriander-Lime Gremolata

A mild, comforting curry with plenty of rich, gooey gravy, ideal for preparing a day ahead of a feast. There's nothing Indian about the gremolata topping, but I'm happy to break the rules here, because it adds a fresh last-minute prickle of flavour.

8 medium lamb shanks
1½ cups (375 ml) thick natural yoghurt
juice of 2 lemons
1 tsp (5 ml) turmeric
1 tsp (5 ml) dried red chilli flakes, or more, to taste
1 tsp (5 ml) salt
3 Tbsp (45 ml) sunflower oil
2 large onions, peeled and finely chopped
8 green cardamom pods
1 small stick of cinnamon
8 dried curry leaves (optional)
5 cloves garlic, peeled and finely chopped
a thumb-size piece fresh ginger, finely grated
8 large ripe tomatoes
1 x 410 g tin chopped Italian tomatoes
2½ cups (675 ml) warm water
2 tsp (10 ml) ground coriander
2 tsp (10 ml) medium-strength curry powder
2 tsp (10 ml) ground cumin
a pinch of ground cloves
1 tsp (5 ml) milled black pepper
a little lemon juice

FOR THE GREMOLATA
2 limes or small lemons
3 cloves garlic, peeled
¾ cup (180 ml) fresh coriander leaves

Cut a few deep slashes in the thickest part of the shanks and place them in a bowl (a big plastic basin is ideal). Whisk together the yoghurt, lemon juice, turmeric, chilli flakes and salt. Pour the marinade over the lamb and rub it deep into the cuts. Set aside in a cool place for 4–5 hours.

Heat the oven to 160 °C. Heat the oil in a large, ovenproof dish, preferably a lidded cast-iron pot. Add the onions, cardamom pods, cinnamon and curry leaves and fry over a medium heat for 5–7 minutes, or until the onions are soft and golden. Stir in the garlic and ginger and cook for another minute, without allowing the garlic to brown. Chop the tomatoes and whizz to a rough slush in a food processor. Pour the tomato pulp over the onions, add the tinned tomatoes and bubble briskly for 12–15 minutes, or until the sauce has darkened and thickened slightly. Stir in the water and all the remaining spices. Season to taste with salt.

Put the lamb shanks and their marinade into the pot and toss everything together so the meat is well coated. Don't worry if the shanks stick up above the gravy line. Cover the pot with its lid or a tight layer of foil, place in the oven and cook for 1 hour. Take off the lid, stir well so every piece of meat is coated, then arrange the shanks upright, bones perpendicular to the base of the pot and thick parts resting in the gravy. Bake, uncovered this time, for another 1¼ hours, or until the meat is fork-tender and beginning to fall away from the bone. Let the pot cool completely, then lift away any solidified fat.

Gently reheat the dish before serving; it will take at least 20 minutes for the shanks to heat right to the bone.

To make the gremolata, finely grate the lime zest, very finely chop the garlic and fresh coriander and gently mix the three together. Squeeze a little lemon juice over the shanks, sprinkle with the gremolata and serve hot on a bed of Basmati rice.

Serves 8.

Notes

This curry benefits from a long mellowing time, so feel confident making it a day or even two days ahead. Lamb shanks are bulky, so you'll need to make this in two separate large pots if you're feeding more than eight people.

Cape Malay-Style Lamb Sosaties with Dried Apricots

This is my modern version of a very old recipe, and one with a bitter-sweet legacy. Spicy kebabs (or 'sesates') were brought to the Cape by slaves from Indonesia and Java, and this recipe has been passed down through many generations to become one of South Africa's most adored braai recipes.

1.8 kg lamb from the leg, cut into large cubes
32 dried apricots
fresh lemon, orange or bay leaves
melted butter for brushing

FOR THE MARINADE
60 g dried tamarind pulp (see Notes)
1 cup (250 ml) boiling water
4 Tbsp (60 ml) sunflower oil
2 large onions, peeled and very finely chopped
4 cardamom pods
1 stick of cinnamon
1 fresh red chilli, deseeded and finely chopped (or more, to taste)
3 Tbsp (45 ml) grated fresh ginger
4 cloves garlic, peeled and finely chopped
2 tsp (10 ml) ground cumin
1 tsp (5 ml) red chilli powder
1½ tsp (7.5 ml) ground coriander
4 Tbsp (60 ml) white wine vinegar
4 Tbsp (60 ml) thick fruit chutney
2 Tbsp (30 ml) sugar
1 Tbsp (15 ml) mild curry powder
1½ tsp (7.5 ml) turmeric
200 ml water
salt and milled black pepper
juice of 1 small lemon
1 cup (250 ml) thick natural yoghurt

Make the marinade first. Put the tamarind in a bowl, cover it with the boiling water and set aside for 10 minutes. Heat the oil in a pan and add the onions, cardamom and cinnamon. Cook over a brisk heat for 5 minutes, or until the onions are soft and golden. Add the chilli, ginger and garlic and cook for another minute, without allowing the garlic to brown. Stir in the cumin, chilli powder, coriander, vinegar and chutney and bubble the sauce for 4 minutes, or until slightly thickened.

Break up the tamarind pulp in the water and tip it into a sieve set over a bowl. Press down on the pulp to extract the juice (discard the pulp). Add the tamarind water to the pan along with the sugar, curry powder, turmeric and water. Season with salt and pepper and simmer for 15 minutes. Remove from the heat, cool to lukewarm and then add the lemon juice and yoghurt. Tip the marinade into a deep non-metallic dish and stir in the lamb cubes. Cover and refrigerate for at least 24 hours, or longer (you can make these up to 2 days in advance).

Soak the apricots in hot water for 15 minutes and drain well. Cut the lemon, orange or bay leaves into pieces the size of a stamp. Thread alternating pieces of lamb, leaves and apricot onto satay sticks. Braai over medium-hot coals, basting frequently with the marinade and a little melted butter, for 10–12 minutes (depending on the heat of your fire), or until the lamb is cooked right through.

To cook them in the oven: heat the grill to its fiercest setting and put the meat on the highest oven rack. Grill the sosaties – turning them once and basting frequently – until the edges of the meat and fruit *just* begin to catch and blacken (this freckling of black is essential for an authentic taste). Move the sosaties to the middle of the oven, turn down the heat to 180 °C and bake until the lamb is cooked through. Serve with yellow rice, a green salad and some Indian pickles.

Serves 8.

Notes

Traditionally, lamb or mutton sosaties included chunks of fat from the sheep's tail, which helped keep the meat juicy. I've replaced the fat with yoghurt, which has a tenderising effect and produces a succulent result. Tamarind pulp is available from spice shops, and can also be bought as a paste, in jars (use about 3 Tbsp/45 ml paste, straight from the jar).

Mike's Youvetsi

This hearty Greek dish of slow-cooked lamb and ripe tomatoes baked with rice-shaped pasta is a great choice for a family feast, not only because it tastes better if it's made a day in advance, but also because it's quite simply delectable. There are many variations of youvetsi, featuring onions, cinnamon, cloves, bay leaves, rosemary, and so on, but this — my version of my friend Mike Karamanof's pared-down recipe — is my favourite, because it tastes of its essential ingredients: lamb and tomatoes.

6 large lamb shanks (see Notes)
3 Tbsp (45 ml) olive oil
juice of 1 large lemon
4 tsp (20 ml) good-quality dried oregano
salt and milled black pepper
10 large, ripe tomatoes
5 cloves garlic, peeled and finely chopped
1.25 litres water
1 cup (250 ml) white wine
1 x 500-g packet orzo or similar rice-shaped pasta
350 g cubed kefalotyri or firm feta cheese (see Notes), plus a little extra, for topping

Heat the oven to 200 °C. Place the lamb shanks in a large, deep roasting pan, pour over the olive oil and sprinkle with the lemon juice, oregano, salt and pepper. Roast, uncovered, for 30 minutes, or until the lamb is nicely browned on top. Peel the tomatoes (p. 99) and finely chop them. Arrange the tomatoes and garlic around the lamb, reduce the heat to 120 °C, and return the dish, uncovered, to the oven.

Slow-roast the lamb for 2–2½ hours, basting occasionally with the pan juices (if you have a fan-assisted oven, switch off the fan). The cooking time will depend on your oven and the size of the lamb shanks: you'll know the meat is ready when it is fork-tender and falling away from the bone.

Pull the meat into large shreds, cover and set aside. Put the roasting pan on the hob over a medium heat. Add the water and wine and bring to the boil, scraping the bottom of the pan to loosen any residue. Add the orzo and cook briskly, stirring occasionally to prevent it sticking, for 12–13 minutes, or until the pasta is cooked and has absorbed most of the liquid. It should be about the consistency of a risotto: not stiff or dry, but not swimming in liquid. Season with salt and pepper and stir in the reserved lamb and the cheese.

Pile the mixture into a large ceramic or glass baking dish (or divide it between smaller dishes) and cover with foil. When you're ready to serve the dish, reheat it in a low oven (about 160 °C) for about 30 minutes. Remove the foil 10–15 minutes before the end of the baking time and scatter some small cubes of cheese on top. Serve hot, with a Greek salad.

Serves 8.

Notes

You can use a whole leg of lamb, or even lamb chops, in this dish, but I prefer shanks because they are lean and flavoursome. If you like, you can marinate the lamb in olive oil, garlic, oregano and lemon juice for a few hours before it goes into the oven. Kefalotyri is a Greek white cheese available from good supermarkets. It has an agreeable firm, dry texture, but is expensive, so feel free to use a combination of kefalotyri and feta, or feta on its own.

Thai-Spiced Pork Fillet with Green Peppercorns and Beans

Many Southeast Asian dishes call for snake beans, Thai basil and green peppercorns on the vine, none of which are commonly available in South Africa. I've come up with a recipe that uses green beans, ordinary basil and brined Madagascan peppercorns to create a vibrant green curry tingling with citrusy flavour. All the mild heat in this dish comes from the peppercorns, which will please guests who don't like chillies.

350 g slim green beans
2 pork fillets, weighing 1.8 kg in total
3 Tbsp (45 ml) sunflower or olive oil
2 x 400 ml tins coconut milk
2 tsp (10 ml) Kikkoman soy sauce
1 Tbsp (15 ml) fish sauce
2 Tbsp (30 ml) fresh lime or lemon juice, or more, to taste
1 cup (250 ml, loosely packed) small fresh basil leaves

FOR THE PASTE
2 stalks fresh lemongrass, lower parts only
3 Tbsp (45 ml) grated fresh ginger
4 cloves garlic, peeled and chopped
6 fresh lime leaves or 8 dried ones, chopped
2 Tbsp (30 ml) chopped fresh coriander roots (see Notes)
5 Tbsp (75 ml) chopped fresh coriander leaves
2 tsp (10 ml) finely grated palm sugar or 1 tsp (5 ml) white sugar
1 tsp (5 ml) ground cumin
7 tsp (35 ml) brined green peppercorns, drained (reserve a few for garnishing)
1 tsp (5 ml) flaky sea salt

First make the paste. Peel and discard the hard outer leaves off the lemongrass stalks, bash the stalks with the back of a heavy knife so they begin to split, then slice them very finely. Using a mortar and pestle (see Notes), pound together all the paste ingredients to form a somewhat coarse pulp. Cover and set aside.

Top and tail the beans and cut them in half or into thirds crossways. Cut the pork fillets into slices about 7 mm thick. Heat the oil in a wok or large, shallow pan and quickly fry the pork slices in three or four batches, over a fierce heat, for a minute or two per batch, or until just beginning to brown. Set aside.

Put a little more oil in the pan, if necessary, add half the spice paste and fry over a medium heat for 1 minute, or until fragrant. Pour in the coconut milk, turn down the heat and simmer for 5 minutes. Return the pork slices to the pan, turn up the heat and bubble briskly for a further 2 minutes. Add the beans, soy sauce, fish sauce and the remaining spice paste.

Cook, stirring, for 3–4 minutes, or until the beans are tender-crisp and bright green and the pork is cooked right through. Stir in the lime juice. Taste the sauce to make sure it has a pleasing balance of salt, sweet and sour, and add more lime juice, soy sauce, sugar and fish sauce, as necessary. Scatter over the basil leaves and a few whole green peppercorns and serve immediately, with rice or noodles.

Serves 8.

Notes

Make this an hour or two in advance, but add the second batch of spice paste, the beans, lime juice and basil just before you serve it. Don't allow the broth to boil wildly, as this may toughen the pork. You can use a mini food processor to make the paste, but I find a mortar and pestle produces a better, less homogenous, result. If you can't find coriander roots, use the stems instead. Add some green chillies to the spice paste if you can't do without them.

Dave's Famous Roast Pork Belly

My uncle, David Walters, master potter of Franschhoek, hand-made the plates, bowls and platters in this book and is internationally respected for his fine craftsmanship. He's famous, too, for this lovely dish of slow-roasted, melting pork belly. No one in my family bothers to compete: Dave has cracked the recipe, and we force him to make it for every important feast.

1 large pork belly, bone in (about 2 kg, or enough for 8; see Notes)
¾ cup (180 ml) olive oil
10 bay leaves, dried or fresh
8 cloves garlic, peeled
milled black pepper
1 Tbsp (15 ml) salt

Score the skin of the belly, not too deeply, into a narrow diamond pattern using a very sharp knife or the blade of a sturdy craft knife. If you're not confident about this, ask your butcher to do it. A few hours before you cook the belly, put the olive oil, bay leaves and garlic into a food processor and whizz to a fairly coarse paste (don't add any salt). Brush the mixture all over the scored skin, pressing it well into the cuts. Grind over plenty of black pepper. Cover with clingfilm and let it stand for 2–3 hours.

Heat the oven to 170 °C. Place the belly, skin-side up, directly onto the middle rack of the oven, and put a pan underneath it to collect the fat. Roast for 3 hours with the oven fan off, and without letting the temperature go above 170 °C (or the skin will crackle prematurely).

After 3 hours the belly will be soft, juicy and well cooked. Fifteen minutes before you want to eat, take the joint out of the oven and use kitchen paper to wipe off any oily puddles on top of the skin. Sprinkle the skin liberally with salt. Turn the top grill of the oven to its highest setting and wait until it is glowing red. Adjust the rack on which you cooked the pork so the skin is about 15 cm below the grill. Within a minute or two the skin will begin to spit and sputter as it forms crackling: watch it like a hawk to make sure it is not burning. If it shows any signs of catching, turn the grill down a little, or move the rack down a notch, but don't remove the pork from the oven. When the crackling is golden and crunchy all over (this will take 8–10 minutes), take the belly out of the oven, put it on a large carving board and take it to the table. Serve with apple sauce, potato salad and a green salad.

Serves 8.

Notes

Order, well in advance, a large slab of top-quality pork belly from your butcher; supermarket pork bellies are of indifferent quality and always too small. If you're throwing caution to the wind, put some parboiled potatoes in the dish underneath the belly an hour or so before you serve it, where they will roast to golden and fatty perfection.

Slow-Cooked Beef Shin Pie with Mushrooms and Rosemary

Long, patient cooking works wonders with inexpensive cuts of beef, and soft shin is my favourite, because it never fails to fall obligingly into melting, fork-tender flakes. This is an easy, earthy dish with simple flavours: use it as a filling for a pie or serve it as is with a mound of creamy mashed potatoes.

45 g dried wild mushrooms, such as shiitake or porcini, or a mixture
1 cup (250 ml) warm water
1.8 kg soft beef shin, bone out
6 Tbsp (90 ml) cake flour
salt and milled black pepper
2 medium onions, peeled and thinly sliced
2 bay leaves
2 x 10-cm sprigs of rosemary
1 cup (250 ml) dry white wine
2 Tbsp (30 ml) sunflower or olive oil
2 Tbsp (30 ml/30 g) butter
750 g portabellini or button mushrooms, or a mixture, halved
4 cloves garlic, peeled and finely grated
½ cup (125 ml) chopped fresh parsley
a little fresh lemon juice

FOR A PIE
1 x 400 g roll readymade puff pastry
1 extra-large free-range egg, lightly beaten

Heat the oven to 160 °C. Soak the dried mushrooms in the warm water for 30 minutes. Trim the fat and any sinew from the shin and cut it into pieces about the size of a deck of cards. Put the flour in a large, lidded cast-iron pot (or similar heavy ovenproof dish) and season it with salt and pepper. Add the shin and toss well so every piece is coated. Fish the dried mushrooms from their soaking liquid and add them to the pot along with the onion rings, bay leaves and one of the rosemary sprigs. Pour ½ cup (125 ml) of the white wine and 1 cup (250 ml) of the mushroom-soaking liquid over the beef and mix everything gently together. Rub a film of oil over the shiny side of a sheet of foil, place it, oiled-side down, on top of the meat, and weigh down with a plate. Cover with a lid and bake for 1¼ hours, without stirring or peeking.

After an hour, start the mushrooms. Heat the oil and butter in a large pan and cook the fresh mushrooms over a medium-high heat for 5 minutes, or until their juices begin to run. Pour in the remaining wine, turn up the heat and cook briskly for a further 3–4 minutes, or until the liquid has reduced slightly. Stir in the garlic. Add the cooked mushrooms and their liquid to the pot, stir well and season to taste with salt and pepper. Remove the rosemary sprig and push the second one deep into the pot. Replace the lid and continue baking at 160 °C for another 1½ hours, or until the meat is falling apart and the sauce is rich, dark and thick. Stir gently now and then, and top up with a little more wine or water if necessary. Remove the rosemary and bay leaves and stir in the parsley and a generous squeeze of lemon juice.

If you're making a pie, tip the filling into a greased dish, cover with puff pastry (p. 115), brush with beaten egg and bake at 180 °C for 30–40 minutes.

Serves 8.

Notes

This can be prepared a day in advance, but if you're making a pie, add the parsley and lemon just before you fill it. You can brown the floured shin and the onions in oil before you add them to the pot, but I don't bother with this any more because I've noticed little difference in the final result. Use bone-in shin for this dish if you like, which will add to its flavour, but remove the bones before you fill the pie.

Roast Pork Neck with Leeks, Carrots and Apples

Pork neck is an inexpensive yet most tender and succulent cut that lends itself to all sorts of interesting flavour combinations. It's not something commonly found on supermarket shelves, but you can order it from any good butcher. I'm a devoted advocate of pork neck, and feel heartened that this dish has held its place, over the years, as one of the all-time most-viewed recipes on my cookery blog.

2 pork necks, weighing about 1 kg each
3 Tbsp (45 ml) wholegrain mustard
3 Tbsp (45 ml) olive oil
juice of ½ lemon
milled black pepper
4 cloves garlic, peeled and sliced

FOR THE VEGETABLES
8 large carrots, peeled
2 Tbsp (30 ml) sunflower oil
1 Tbsp (15 ml/15 g) butter
8 large leeks, white and pale green parts only, sliced
2 onions, peeled and quartered
4 Golden Delicious apples or similar firm, sweet apples
3 cloves garlic, peeled and chopped
1 Tbsp (15ml) fresh thyme leaves
3 Tbsp (45 ml) sliced fresh sage leaves
salt and milled black pepper
¾ cup (180 ml) water or stock
¾ cup (180 ml) white wine

FOR THE GRAVY
4 tsp (20 ml) cake flour
2 cups (500 ml) stock or a combination of stock and white wine

Heat the oven to 200 °C. Place the pork necks in a roasting pan and smear all over with mustard. Sprinkle with olive oil and lemon juice and season with pepper. Tuck the garlic slices under the pork. Place the pan on the middle rack of the oven and roast for 35 minutes, or until the pork is golden on top.

In the meantime, prepare the vegetables. Top and tail the carrots and cut into thick batons. Heat the oil and butter in a large, shallow pan and add the carrots, leeks and onions. Cook over a high heat for 6–8 minutes, or until the leeks and onions begin to colour. Core the apples, cut each into eight wedges and add them to the pan along with the chopped garlic, thyme and sage. Cook, tossing, for another 3 minutes, then season with salt and pepper.

Lift the pork necks and drain any excess fat from the pan. Spread the vegetables over the base of the pan and put the pork necks on top. Pour over the water (or stock) and the white wine. Reduce the heat to 150 °C and roast, uncovered, for 1½ hours, or until the vegetables are soft and the pork tender. Remove the pork, vegetables (put a few spoonfuls of carrots and onions back into the pan) and any juices from the pan and place on a large platter. Cover with foil and keep warm.

To make the gravy, place the pan on the hob and turn up the heat. Sprinkle the flour into the pan and stir well, scraping to dislodge any residue. Cook for 2 minutes, pressing down on the onions and carrots with the back of a spoon. Pour in the stock and bubble over a gentle heat until the gravy thickens. Strain the gravy into a warmed jug. Carve the pork into thick slices and serve immediately with the vegetables and gravy.

Serves 8.

Notes

Check the dish every now and then while it's roasting and top up with a little stock, if necessary; by the end of the cooking time, there should be just a few tablespoons of liquid left in the pan. If you'd like some rich colour in the gravy, add a splash of soy sauce; for extra sweetness, add a tablespoonful of cranberry jelly.

Corned Beef in Broth with Baby Vegetables and Two Sauces

This is an updated version of what my mum calls 'Boiled Beef and Carrots'. She always sang this old music-hall ditty when she served this favourite comfort meal of both our childhoods, and I can't think of a more soul-nourishing dish for a winter's feast. It's a plain – even frugal-tasting – dish, with a voluptuous cloak of flavoured béchamel adding a necessary layer of luxury. Because I can never decide whether I prefer a parsley or a mustard sauce, I now always make both.

1 x 2.2 kg piece corned (pickled) beef
½ onion, studded with 3 whole cloves
2 bay leaves
a few sprigs of fresh thyme
8 stalks parsley (reserve the leaves)
3 ripe tomatoes, halved
1 stalk celery
1 tsp (5 ml) black peppercorns
1 kg tiny new potatoes
32 baby carrots
32 pencil-thin baby leeks
350 g slim green beans, topped and tailed

FOR THE BÉCHAMEL
4 Tbsp (60 ml/60 g) butter
4 Tbsp (60 ml) cake flour
3 cups (750 ml) cold milk
½ cup (125 ml) fresh cream
salt and a pinch or two of white pepper
lemon juice, to taste

FOR THE PARSLEY SAUCE
½ cup (125 ml) finely chopped curly parsley
1 Tbsp (15 ml) finely chopped capers

FOR THE MUSTARD SAUCE
2 Tbsp (30 ml) Dijon mustard
2 Tbsp (30 ml) wholegrain mustard
milled black pepper

Put the beef into a large pot, cover it with water and bring to the boil, skimming off the foam as it rises. Now drain off the water, rinse the pot and cover the meat with fresh water. Add the onion, bay leaves, thyme, parsley stalks, tomatoes, celery and peppercorns. Weigh down the meat with a small plate, cover the pot with a tilted lid and bring up to a gentle simmer. Cook very gently – the water should barely burble – for 1½–2 hours, or until the meat is very tender (see Notes).

Make a thick béchamel sauce (p. 188) using the butter, flour and milk. Add just enough hot stock (about 100–150 ml) from the pot to dilute the sauce to a thick pouring consistency, and bubble for a further 3–4 minutes. Remove from the heat, stir in the cream, season with salt and white pepper and add a spritz of lemon juice to sharpen it. Divide the mixture between two bowls. To one, add the chopped parsley and capers; to the other, the two mustards and some black pepper. Cover the surfaces of the sauces with clingfilm and set aside.

About 25 minutes before serving, strain off the stock, leaving the meat in the warm pot with the lid on. Pour half the stock into a new pot (save the remaining stock for a future soup) and bring to the boil. Add the new potatoes and simmer briskly for 10 minutes. Then add the carrots and leeks and cook for another 7–8 minutes, or until the vegetables are almost soft, but nowhere near mushy. Finally, add the green beans and cook for 3–4 minutes, until tender but still bright green.

Cut the beef into thick slices – or pull it apart into chunks, as you please – and heap them in the middle of a large warmed platter. Arrange the vegetables around the edges and trickle over some of the stock in which you cooked them. Serve immediately, and pass the reheated sauces round in separate jugs.

Serves 8.

Notes

The meat can be cooked in advance, cooled in its liquid and then gently heated through, but slice it and boil the vegetables just before you serve the dish.

Individual Beef Wellingtons with Crisp Bottoms

A soggy-bottomed Beef Wellington is very off-putting, but if you are prepared to take the time to follow this recipe carefully, you are assured of success, and will be serving what to me is the epitome of a luxurious feast dish. Add a thin layer of chicken liver pâté to the stacks if you want to go the whole hog; I leave it out because there's bound to be someone at the table who doesn't like it.

1 large (about 1.8 kg) fillet of beef or 8 x 5 cm-thick fillet medallions
3 x 400 g rolls readymade puff pastry, thawed
1 extra-large free-range egg, lightly beaten with 1 tsp (5 ml) water
4 tsp (20 ml) Dijon mustard
milled black pepper
2 Tbsp (30 ml) olive oil
2 Tbsp (30 ml/30 g) butter
650 g portabellini or button mushrooms, finely chopped
a large sprig of fresh rosemary
3 Tbsp (45 ml) dry white wine
2 cloves garlic, peeled and finely chopped

Trim the fillet, removing the thin 'tail', and wrap it lengthways in a 75-cm sheet of clingfilm. Twirl the ends tightly, as if you are making a Christmas cracker, and continue twisting until you have a neat, tight, evenly thick roll. Refrigerate for at least 6 hours. Slice the fillet, straight through the clingfilm, into eight medallions, each about 5 cm thick. Peel off the clingfilm.

Heat the oven to 220 °C. Roll out a sheet of pastry so it's 2 cm bigger on all sides. Cut out six circles 1 cm bigger in diameter than the fillet medallions. Cut two more circles from the second roll of pastry. Prick the pastry with a fork, place on a baking sheet lined with baking paper and bake for 8–10 minutes, or until light gold. Brush the discs with egg and return to the oven for 4–5 minutes, or until golden brown and dry to the touch. Cool on a wire rack.

Smear the medallions with mustard and black pepper. Heat the oil in a pan until it's so hot it shimmers. Sear the steaks, in batches, for exactly 1 minute on each side; they should be nicely browned but still raw inside. Add the butter, mushrooms and rosemary to the pan and fry over a medium heat for 4–5 minutes, or until the juices run. Add the wine and garlic and bubble until the liquid has evaporated. Remove the rosemary, season and set aside to cool. Divide the mushroom mixture into eight portions and pat a layer onto each pastry disc. Place a medallion on top and season with salt. Cut eight large circles from the remaining pastry (big enough to cover the stacks completely). Drape the circles over the stacks and tuck the edges under the cooked pastry discs. Brush with egg and cut a small slit in the top. Bake at 200 °C on a baking sheet lined with baking paper. For medium-rare steak, bake for about 20 minutes (see Notes). Serve hot with a sauce of your choice.

Serves 8.

Notes

You can make up the parcels up to 24 hours ahead and refrigerate them, but make sure the meat and mushrooms are cold when you assemble the stacks. Bring them up to room temperature before baking. To test for doneness, push the tines of a fork deep into one of the pastry stacks, leave for 30 seconds and hold the tines to your upper lip. If they're hot, the fillet is medium-rare. For a bloody steak, cook for about 15 minutes; for well done, 25–30 minutes.

Beef Fillet with Mash, Rocket and a Balsamic Glaze

In my house, this recipe is reserved for very grand occasions, not only because fillet is ruinously expensive, but also because my family love it so dearly. I keep them on short rations (so to speak) because I fear that if I make it too often, their faces will no longer light up with joy when I announce we're having *that* dish for supper.

1 fillet of beef big enough to serve 8 people, or two smaller ones (about 1.8 kg)
2 Tbsp (30 ml) Dijon mustard
2 Tbsp (30 ml) Kikkoman soy sauce
4 Tbsp (60 ml) olive oil
milled black pepper
2 Tbsp (30 ml/30 g) butter
5 Tbsp (75 ml) water or stock
½ cup (125 ml) balsamic vinegar
350 g (or enough for 8 people) fresh rocket leaves
1 x 150 g wedge Parmesan or Grana Padano

FOR THE MASH
12 large floury potatoes, peeled and quartered
butter and milk for mashing
salt and milled black pepper

FOR THE DRESSING
juice of 1 large lemon
4 Tbsp (60 ml) extra-virgin olive oil

Trim the fillet of any sinew and place it in a dish. Smear the mustard, soy sauce and 1 Tbsp (15 ml) of the olive oil over the meat and season with black pepper. Cover and set aside for an hour or two at room temperature.

Cook the potatoes in salted, boiling water for 25 minutes, or until quite tender. Drain in a colander for 5 minutes, then return to the pan and mash with a little butter and milk until smooth. Season with salt and pepper, cover and keep hot.

Heat the oven to 190 °C. Set a large, shallow pan over a fierce heat and add the remaining 3 Tbsp (45 ml) of olive oil. When the oil begins to shimmer, quickly sear the fillet on all sides; this should take no longer than 4 or 5 minutes. Stir in the butter after a few minutes and baste the fillet with the pan juices as it fries. Slide the fillet onto a baking sheet, season with a little salt, if necessary, and roast for 15–25 minutes, or until done to your liking (see Notes). Turn the heat on again under the pan, add the water and stir briskly to dislodge any sediment. Pour in the balsamic vinegar and bubble over a medium heat for a few minutes, or until the liquid has reduced by about half to a slightly syrupy glaze.

Pile the rocket leaves into a bowl and dress them with the lemon juice and olive oil. Take the fillet out of the oven, cover and allow to rest for 5–8 minutes. Carve the meat into slices 1 cm thick. Pile a heap of hot mashed potato into the centres of eight warmed plates. Place a few slices of fillet on each plate and drizzle over a little of the balsamic glaze. Crown each pile of mash with a tuft of dressed rocket, and use a potato peeler to shave over thin flakes of Parmesan. Drizzle over a little more olive oil and serve immediately.

Serves 8.

Notes

This dish requires some split-second timing, but you can make the mashed potatoes and sear the fillet (without baking it) a few hours in advance. Keep the browned fillet, uncovered, in the fridge and bring it up to room temperature before you finish roasting it. For a perfect, rosy pink result, leave the fillet (if it's a large, single fillet) in the oven for 15–17 minutes, then use the fork-to-lip method (see Beef Wellington, p. 146) to test for doneness. Alternatively, you can cut a sneaky slit in the deepest part of the fillet to check for doneness, although you may lose some of the juices this way.

Spicy Frikkadels with Minted Couscous

I don't normally serve mince at special feasts because it just doesn't seem very festive, but this dish is an exception, pairing a minty couscous salad with hot, lightly spiced meatballs and a lemony dressing. You can use beef, pork or lamb mince for these; I find that half beef and half pork produces the juiciest frikkadels. This is lovely served with dollops of cold, creamy tzatziki.

2 extra-large free-range eggs
6 Tbsp (90 ml) thick natural yoghurt
1½ cups (375 ml) fresh white breadcrumbs
1.25 kg minced beef, lamb or pork
1 small onion, peeled and grated
3 cloves garlic, peeled and crushed
⅓ cup (80 ml) finely chopped fresh coriander
1½ tsp (7.5 ml) ground coriander
1½ tsp (7.5 ml) ground cumin
finely grated zest of 1 lemon
salt and milled black pepper
½ cup (125 ml) chickpea flour
1 tsp (5 ml) turmeric
½ tsp (2.5 ml) paprika
4 Tbsp (60 ml) sunflower oil, for frying

FOR THE COUSCOUS
3 cups (about 500 g) couscous
juice and finely grated zest of 1 large lemon
juice and finely grated zest of 1 orange
¾ cup (180 ml) light olive oil
1 Tbsp (15 ml) paprika
2 Tbsp (30 ml) dried mint
1½ tsp (7.5 ml) ground cumin
¾ cup (180 ml) finely chopped fresh mint
½ cup (125 ml) shelled pistachio nuts
sprigs of fresh coriander

Whisk the egg and yoghurt in a large mixing bowl, stir in the breadcrumbs and leave to soak for 5 minutes. Add the mince, grated onion, garlic, fresh and ground coriander, cumin, lemon zest and salt and black pepper to taste. Using your hands, squish everything together to make a fairly firm paste. Test the seasoning by frying a little patty in hot oil; taste it, and add more salt, pepper and spice, as required. Roll the paste into meatballs, each about the size of a litchi. Chill for 30 minutes.

Put the couscous into a large bowl and cover, to a depth of about 7 mm, with warm water (see Notes). Leave for 12 minutes, or until all the water has been absorbed, then fluff the grains with a fork to separate them. In another bowl, whisk together the lemon and orange zest and juice, the oil, paprika, dried mint and cumin and season generously with salt. Pour three-quarters of the dressing over the warm couscous and toss well. Cool to room temperature, stir in the fresh mint and pile onto a large platter, or two smaller ones. Make a large well in the middle.

Mix the chickpea flour, turmeric and paprika on a plate. Roll the meatballs in the flour and dust off the excess. Fry in hot oil, in batches, for 3–4 minutes, or until crusty and golden, and cooked right through; don't allow the meatballs to burn. Set aside.

Pile the meatballs onto the couscous and pour over the remaining dressing. Sprinkle with the pistachio nuts and coriander sprigs and serve immediately.

Serves 8.

Notes

Roll the meatballs up to 24 hours ahead and keep covered in the fridge. Make the couscous a few hours ahead, too, and keep covered at room temperature, but add the fresh mint and pistachios at the last minute. Although they're best fresh from the pan, the meatballs can be fried an hour or so ahead and gently reheated in the pan in which you cooked them. My method of using very warm (not boiling) water to make the couscous results in fluffy grains, but you will need to use an 'instant' or 'quick-cook' brand.

Desserts

My number-one criterion in choosing a dessert for a feast is that it can be prepared the day before. Of course delicious-ness enters into the equation, but being able to make the sweet course well in advance is crucial to me. By the time the end of a meal arrives, I want to put my feet up, let my hair down and enjoy the rest of the party.

Of course, this isn't always achievable, especially in the dreariest days of winter, when a hot, cakey pudding cloaked in custard is called for. In this case, I will choose a pud that is quick and easy to sling together and needs little or no last-minute attention.

I am not much of a pudding eater and don't make them very often, so I was guided when writing this chapter by the precise requirements of my dessert-deprived family. My husband yearns for the delights of his English childhood: steamed puddings, fruit crumbles and tart, berry-filled pies. My children, now in their teens, demand ice cream, chocolate, trifles, hot fudgy puddings and cheesecake. And when I asked a variety of sweet-toothed friends what they'd most like to eat at the end of a special feast, I was surprised to find out how many pooh-poohed 'cheffy' desserts and expressed a longing for the simple puds of yesteryear, notably comforting nursery puddings and ones made with condensed milk, jelly and tinned fruit. 'I want trashy puddings,' one friend told me. 'I don't eat them often, so when I do, I expect the Full Monty: glacé cherries, booze, chocolate shavings and all.' This confirmed my belief that most people don't expect anything clever in a pudding; what they really want is pure eating pleasure.

So indulgence is the key here: there's no room for calorie counting when it comes to a proper feast. There are a few light, fruity desserts in this chapter, for the very hottest of days, but the rest are laden with cream, chocolate, butter, alcohol and all the other gorgeous things a good pudding promises.

There are five recipes involving ice cream in this chapter, because everybody loves it and, besides, it is the perfect dessert to make a day or two ahead of your feast. None of these recipes requires an ice-cream churn or laborious beating: mix 'em, freeze 'em and forget about 'em is my motto.

With desserts, it's vital to measure everything precisely, especially when it comes to tricky ingredients such as baking powder, gelatine and essences. All the tarts in this chapter yield eight decent-size slices, but if you're expecting a bunch of pudding fanatics, it might be wise to make two of a particular recipe.

Cape Gooseberry Meringue Pie

My twist on a much-loved family pud, this pie is wonderfully tart and crammed with intense gooseberry flavour. This is an unusual recipe because a gelatine filling is briefly heated in the oven while the meringue is browning. Measure everything exactly and you can't go wrong.

4 cups (about 650 g) dehusked Cape gooseberries
½ cup (125 ml) caster sugar
½ cup (125 ml) water
2½ tsp (12.5 ml) cornflour
juice of ½ lemon
1 Tbsp (15 ml) powdered gelatine

FOR THE BISCUIT CRUST
1 x 200 g packet Tennis biscuits or similar crumbly coconut biscuits
6 Tbsp (90 ml/90 g) very soft butter

FOR THE TOPPING
4 extra-large free-range egg whites
a pinch of salt
1 cup (250 ml) caster sugar

First make the crust. Break up the biscuits and process them to fine crumbs in a food processor. Place in a bowl with the soft butter and stir well to combine. Lightly press the mixture onto the base of a non-stick 24-cm springform cake pan lined with buttered baking paper (or use your favourite pie dish). Chill the crust while you make the filling.

Put the gooseberries, caster sugar and water into a pan, turn on the heat and simmer, stirring occasionally, for 6–8 minutes, or until the berries are just beginning to collapse. Mix the cornflour and lemon juice until smooth, add this to the gooseberries and cook, stirring, for 2 minutes or until slightly thickened. Remove from the heat and cool for a few minutes. Now sprinkle the gelatine evenly all over the hot liquid and stir until it has completely dissolved. Cool for 15 minutes, then pour the mixture over the prepared crust. Refrigerate for 1½ hours.

Heat the oven to 190 °C. Beat the egg whites with the salt until very firm, but not dry. Add 1 Tbsp (15 ml) of the caster sugar and beat again until firm. Add the remaining caster sugar gradually, beating all the time until you have a very stiff, glossy meringue. Pile the meringue over the gooseberry filling and, using the back of the spoon, coax it towards the edges of the tin, making sure there is a tight seal. Bake for 5–7 minutes, or until the meringue is a light coffee colour. Cool for 20 minutes, then refrigerate for at least 4 hours, or longer. Serve cold.

Makes one 24-cm pie; serves 8.

Notes

Take your time beating the meringue to a shiny, billowing cloud; this should take you at least 4–5 minutes. Don't be tempted to run a knife round the edges of the meringue until you are about to release the pie from the cake pan for serving, as it will shrink back from the edges.

Nougat and Ice Cream Cake with Hot Raspberry Sauce

My aunt Gilly Walters, a superlative cook and the inventive brain behind one of South Africa's best-loved nougats, showed me this method of adding whipped cream and chopped frozen nougat to good shop-bought vanilla ice cream. What I love about ice-cream cakes like this is that they look spectacular and are so versatile: you can add anything that takes your fancy to the mix — chopped dark chocolate, nuts, liqueur, and so on.

FOR THE BISCUIT CRUST
1 x 200 g packet shortbread biscuits
6 Tbsp (90 ml/90 g) very soft butter

FOR THE FILLING AND SAUCE
2 litres full-cream vanilla ice cream
1 x 110 g bar nutty nougat, frozen solid
10 Romany Creams or similar chocolate biscuit
1 cup (250 ml) or 1 x 250 ml tub fresh cream
3 cups (750 ml) frozen raspberries
about 3 Tbsp (45 ml) icing sugar (see Notes)
a little lemon juice

Take the ice cream out of the freezer and let it soften slightly. In the meantime, whizz the shortbread biscuits to a fairly fine crumb in a food processor. Place in a bowl, add the soft butter and stir well to combine. Wet the base of a non-stick 24-cm springform cake pan and cover with clingfilm. Tuck the edges of the plastic under the base, pulling it quite tight as you fasten it in the ring. Press the biscuit mixture evenly onto the lined base and refrigerate it while you make the filling.

Using a heavy knife, chop the frozen nougat bar into pea-size pieces and cut the chocolate biscuits into big chunks. Whip the cream to a soft peak in a large bowl and, working quickly so the mixture doesn't melt, fold in the slightly softened ice cream, nougat, biscuits and half the frozen raspberries. Tip the mixture over the crumb crust and, using a spatula, swirl the top into generous waves and ripples. Cover and freeze.

Put the remaining raspberries, the icing sugar and a squeeze of lemon juice (see Notes) in a small pan, bring to a gentle simmer and cook for 2–3 minutes, stirring occasionally. Using a stick blender or food processor, whizz to a purée. Strain the sauce if you'd like it fine, or leave it slightly rough. Set aside to reheat later.

Loosen the edges of the ice-cream cake by briefly pressing a hot kitchen cloth against the sides (p. 159). Slip a spatula or palette knife between the crumb base and the clingfilm and loosen it by using gentle levering movements, turning the pan as you go. Slide the cake onto a plate or cake stand, leaving the base and clingfilm behind. Cut the cake into slices using a knife dipped in very hot water, and serve with the hot raspberry sauce.

Makes one 24-cm cake; serves 8.

Notes

Choose a proper dairy ice cream for this cake, not the frozen 'desserts' that pass for vanilla ice cream. Let the cake stand at room temperature for 5–10 minutes, or until just soft enough to slice. How much lemon juice and icing sugar you add to the raspberry sauce will depend on how tart or sweet they are to begin with; adjust as necessary.

Lemon Curd Mousse

This dessert is the result of a happy accident: one day, in a distracted mood, I mistakenly left two ingredients out of another jelly recipe I was attempting. The result needed some tweaking, but several tries later I had a buttercup-yellow mousse with a lovely lemon curd taste. This is fairly quick to make, because you don't need to sponge and melt the gelatine separately.

8 extra-large free-range egg yolks
6 extra-large free-range egg whites
1 cup (250 ml) white sugar
1 Tbsp (15 ml) powdered gelatine
½ tsp (2.5 ml) cornflour
finely grated zest of 2 lemons
4 Tbsp (60 ml) lemon juice (you'll need 2 big lemons)
1 cup (250 ml) fresh cream, chilled
a pinch of salt

Separate the eggs and set the 6 egg whites to one side. Put the yolks, sugar, gelatine, cornflour, lemon zest and juice into a metal bowl and whisk for 1 minute, until creamy. Place the bowl over a pan of simmering water (the bowl should fit snugly, and its base must not touch the water). Cook, stirring continuously with the whisk, until the mixture is very hot and slightly thickened. This will take 5 or 6 minutes, and you will find that the mixture thickens quite suddenly (at 71–73 °C, if you have a cooking thermometer), at which point remove it immediately from the heat. Don't let the mixture get too hot, or it may curdle.

Whisk in the chilled cream and strain the mixture into a clean bowl. Whisk the egg whites with a pinch of salt to a firm (but nowhere near dry) peak. Add a big blob of whites to the mixture to slacken it, stir well, then very gently fold in the remaining egg whites. Divide the mixture between eight glasses, then cover and chill for 4–5 hours, or until firm. Serve with fresh fruit.

Serves 8.

Notes

If you would like a whole moulded mousse, use 5 tsp (25 ml) gelatine. The easiest way to release a set pudding from its mould is to wet a kitchen cloth and put it in the microwave to heat for 30–45 seconds. Put a serving plate face-down on top of the pudding, then quickly flip it over to invert it. Briefly press the hot cloth against the sides of the mould, reheating the cloth once if necessary. Give the jelly a shake and a smart tap, and it should plop obligingly onto the plate.

White Coffee-Bean Panna Cotta with Chocolate Sauce

Your guests will be surprised to find that these lovely white, wobbly creams are infused with a rich coffee flavour. You can serve them as is, or with a trickle of chocolate sauce. For best results, measure the cream, milk and gelatine with great care.

600 ml fresh cream
600 ml full-cream milk
6 Tbsp (90 ml) whole roasted coffee beans
200 ml caster sugar
3 Tbsp (45 ml) tepid water
3 or 4 tsp (15 or 20 ml) gelatine, depending
on how you present the panna cottas
(see Notes)

FOR THE SAUCE
65 ml warm water
100 g dark chocolate (75% cocoa solids)

Put the cream, milk, coffee beans and caster sugar into a saucepan, over a low heat, and bring gradually to just below the boil, stirring now and then to dissolve the sugar. When the mixture starts to seethe and rise in the pan, take it off the heat and cover the cream's surface with a piece of clingfilm. Cool, shaking the pan occasionally, for an hour or longer, or until it reaches room temperature. (The longer you leave the beans to infuse, the stronger the coffee taste will be. Taste the mixture before you add the gelatine.)

Put the water into a small teacup or ramekin and sprinkle over the gelatine (for quantity, see Notes). Set aside to sponge for 3 minutes. Now put the cup into a pan of simmering water (the water should come halfway up its sides) and leave it there, without stirring, until all the gelatine has melted and the liquid is clear. Stir it into the cream, making sure every bit of liquid goes in ('rinse' the cup out in the hot cream). Strain the cream through a fine sieve into eight lightly oiled or sprayed ramekin dishes (if you want moulded puddings) or glasses (if you'd like a more wobbly set). Chill for 6 hours, or overnight.

To make the sauce, put the water into a metal bowl set over a pan of simmering water. Grate the chocolate coarsely and add it, bit by bit, to the hot water, stirring gently until it has melted and the sauce is smooth. Unmould the panna cottas (p. 159) and serve them with just-warm chocolate sauce.

Serves 8.

Notes

If you're going to serve this in glasses, use exactly 1 Tbsp (15 ml) of powdered gelatine. If you'd like to make moulded panna cottas that will just hold their own shape, use 4 tsp (20 ml) gelatine. Buy the best-quality roast coffee beans you can afford.

Frozen Lemon Cream with Summer Berries

Lemony condensed milk mixed with whipped cream is one of South Africa's more popular pie fillings – not surprising because it's delicious and easy to make. There is no gelatine in the mixture, which relies on a reaction between the condensed milk and the acid in fresh lemon juice to thicken it. In this quick, simple dessert, I've frozen the lemon cream with berries and Amaretti biscuits to create a pretty parfait.

2 cups (500 ml) or 2 x 385 g tins condensed milk
finely grated zest and juice of 3 medium lemons
2 cups (500 ml) or 2 x 250 ml tubs fresh cream
350 g mixed frozen berries
12 Italian Amaretti biscuits

FOR THE TOPPING
1 cup (250 ml) frozen berries, thawed, or fresh ones in season
icing sugar, for dusting

Tip the condensed milk into a large bowl and stir in the lemon zest and juice. Beat at a low speed with a rotary beater for 1 minute, or until slightly thickened. Turn the beater to its highest speed and add the cream in a steady trickle. Once you've added all the cream, continue beating for another minute, or until the mixture is thick and very fluffy. Don't over-beat, or the cream may split. Alternatively, you can whip the cream separately and then fold it into the condensed milk mixture.

Set the mixture aside for 10 minutes to thicken. Partially thaw the berries for 15 minutes in a colander (see Notes). Slice any big berries, such as strawberries, into small pieces. Line a large loaf pan or a cake pan with clingfilm, pressing it well into the edges and corners (wet the pan first, which will help the clingfilm to stick). Spread a third of the cream mixture over the bottom of the pan and top with half of the berries. Roughly crumble the biscuits, then sprinkle half of them over the berries. Spread another third of the cream mixture over the top and top with the remaining berries and crumbled biscuits. Spread the last third of the lemon cream over the top and smooth with a spatula. Cover the surface with a sheet of clingfilm and freeze for 6–7 hours, or overnight.

Invert the pan on a chilled serving platter to unmould the dessert and peel off the clingfilm. Top with a selection of whole berries, dust with a little icing sugar and take straight to the table. Cut into thick slices using a hot knife and serve on cold plates. This is also good with raspberry sauce (p. 156).

Serves 8.

Notes

You can use fresh berries for this parfait, when they're in season. Amaretti biscuits are available from Italian delis and good supermarkets. Take a jug of hot water to the table with you so you can dip the knife in it every now and then.

Steamed Ginger Pudding

My husband's eyes still turn misty when he remembers the steamed puddings made by his late mother, who was an excellent, intuitive and thoroughly English cook. I'm sorry I never asked her for this recipe, but I hope the version I've figured out comes close.

100 ml golden syrup
4 Tbsp (60 ml) finely chopped preserved ginger
1 Tbsp (15 ml) syrup from the ginger jar
juice of 1 large lemon
200 g butter, softened
1⅓ cups (330 ml) white sugar
4 extra-large free-range eggs
1⅓ cups (330 ml) cake flour
5 tsp (25 ml) ground ginger
1½ tsp (7.5 ml) baking powder
a pinch of salt
a little milk (see recipe)
2 Tbsp (30 ml) very finely grated lemon zest

Put a large, heavy-bottomed pan on the heat, add about 7 cm depth of water and bring to the boil. Butter a sturdy glass pudding bowl (or a thick-walled ceramic dish) with a capacity of about 1.5 litres. Cut a circle of foil big enough to cover the bowl and overlap the edges by at least 5 cm. Pour the golden syrup into the bottom of the bowl and add the ginger pieces and the ginger syrup from the jar. Squeeze over the lemon juice, but do not stir. Set aside.

Put the soft butter and sugar into a large mixing bowl and beat with an electric mixer until light and fluffy. Add the eggs, one by one, beating well between each addition. Sift over the flour, ginger, baking powder and salt. Starting at one side of the bowl, gradually incorporate the dry ingredients into the butter/sugar mixture, adding just enough milk (3–5 Tbsp/45–75 ml is usually enough) as you go to achieve a soft, dropping consistency. Stir in the lemon zest.

Pour the batter into the pudding bowl, taking care not to disturb the syrup. Don't fill the bowl to its brim: the batter should be at least 2 cm clear of the rim. Cover with the foil, pressing its overlapping edge down over the outside of the bowl. Secure the foil with a piece of kitchen string, tying it below the lip of the bowl, and knot tightly. Put the bowl into the pan of boiling water: the water should reach halfway up the sides of the bowl. Cover the pan with a lid. Cook, keeping the water at a gentle, burbling boil, for 1½–2 hours, or until the surface is puffed and firm to the touch. Top up the pan with water as necessary. Run a knife around the edges of the pudding to loosen it, then invert it onto a heated plate.

Serve with warm custard or cold whipped cream, or both.

Serves 8.

Notes

To ring the changes, use a mild-tasting honey instead of golden syrup, or a mixture of honey and golden syrup. This pudding is best as it comes out of the pot, but you can steam it in advance, set it aside to cool, then reheat it, unopened, in the same pot of water (reheating will take 15–20 minutes). Make a generous pleat in the circle of the foil to allow for expansion, and – for ease of lifting the pudding from its water bath – make a 'handle' using a double length of string, attached on either side to the string securing the foil.

Almond and Coconut Tart

I love this almondy tart, a favourite recipe from my mum. With its classic pâté brisée crust and frangipane filling, it's sinfully rich and buttery – the least I expect from a dessert that finishes off a grand feast. Ring the changes by pressing wafer-thin slices of apple, nectarine, peach or plum into the filling before you bake it.

FOR THE PASTRY
200 g cake flour
180 g cold butter
a pinch of salt
1 extra-large free-range egg yolk
2–3 Tbsp (30–45 ml) iced water

FOR THE FILLING
100 g softened butter
½ cup (125 ml) caster sugar
2 extra-large free-range eggs, lightly beaten
1 cup (250 ml) ground almonds
¾ cup (180 ml) desiccated coconut
2 Tbsp (30 ml) self-raising flour
1 tsp (5 ml) almond extract or essence
2 Tbsp (30 ml) smooth apricot jam, plus extra for brushing
4 Tbsp (60 ml) toasted flaked almonds, for decorating (optional)

To make the pastry, put the flour, butter and salt into a food processor fitted with a metal blade. Process until the mixture resembles fine breadcrumbs then, with the motor running at low speed, tip in the egg yolk. Now add the iced water in small trickles, pressing the pulse button a few times as you do so, until the pastry *just* holds together in a loose ball. Tip the pastry onto a board and press it very lightly together with your fingertips, without kneading it. Pat into a 4-cm-thick disc, wrap in clingfilm and place in the fridge for 20 minutes.

Heat the oven to 180 °C. Grease a non-stick 24-cm flan pan or pie dish. Roll out the pastry into a circle (see Notes) about 3–4 mm thick and 6 cm bigger all round than your pie dish. Line the dish with the pastry, pressing it lightly into the corners and allowing the edges to drape over the sides of the dish (you'll remove the overlapping pastry later). Prick the pastry base and bake blind (see Notes).

For the filling, cream the butter and sugar. Whisk in the egg, a little at a time, then add the ground almonds, coconut, flour and almond extract and stir well. Warm the jam and spread it thinly over the base of the pastry. Pour the filling over the jam, smooth the top and press the toasted flaked almonds lightly into the mixture. If you're baking this with slices of fruit, press them lightly, in overlapping circles, into the filling. Bake for 20–25 minutes, or until golden and slightly puffed. If the pastry edges seem to be browning too fast, cover them loosely with strips of foil. Remove the tart from the oven and run a knife around the edges of the tart, chipping away the overhanging pastry as you do so. Brush the fruit, if you're using it, with a little melted apricot jam. Serve warm with whipped cream or crème fraîche, or vanilla ice cream.

Makes one 24-cm tart; serves 8.

Notes

The easiest way to deal with sticky pastry is to roll it out between two sheets (or several overlapping squares) of clingfilm. To bake the pastry blind, line it with a circle of baking paper or foil and weigh down with 2 cups (500 ml) of lentils, dried beans or rice. Bake at 180 °C for 10 minutes, then remove the paper and lentils and bake for a further 5–7 minutes, or until the base is dry to the touch. You can get away without blind-baking the pastry, but it will be slightly soggy underneath. Knocking off the overlapping edges *after* baking prevents the pastry from shrinking back and creates a nice even edge.

Hazelnut and Chocolate Cheesecake

A chocolatey, nutty biscuit base, a dash of nutty liqueur and a topping of scribbled dark chocolate give this easy unbaked cheesecake a decadent touch.

FOR THE BISCUIT BASE

5 Tbsp (75 ml) whole hazelnuts, plus extra for decorating

1 x 200 g packet chocolate digestive biscuits

6 Tbsp (90 ml/90 g) very soft butter

FOR THE CHEESECAKE

4 tsp (20 ml) powdered gelatine

¼ cup (60 ml) tepid water

2 x 250 g tubs full-fat cream cheese

1 cup (250 ml) caster sugar

2 Tbsp (30 ml) Frangelico hazelnut liqueur or a similar liqueur of your choice

1 vanilla pod or 1 tsp (5 ml) vanilla extract

1 cup (250 ml) or 1 x 250 ml tub fresh cream

FOR THE TOPPING

75 g dark chocolate (75% cocoa solids), broken into pieces

Put the hazelnuts in a dry frying pan and toss for a few minutes over medium heat, or until lightly toasted. Wrap the nuts in a clean tea towel and rub them between your hands to remove the skins (don't worry if bits of skin remain here and there). Break up the biscuits and place them, with the cooled hazelnuts, in a food processor. Whizz to coarse crumbs, but don't over-process, which will make the chocolate sticky and the nuts oily. Place in a bowl, add the soft butter and stir well to combine. Press the mixture evenly onto the base of a non-stick 24-cm springform cake pan lined with clingfilm (p. 156). Refrigerate while you make the filling.

Sponge the gelatine in the water, then melt it (p. 160). Set aside to cool for a few minutes. Combine the cream cheese, caster sugar and hazelnut liqueur in a large bowl and whisk for 1 minute until smooth. Cut the vanilla pod in half, scrape out the black seeds and add them to the bowl. Stir in the warm gelatine mixture. Whip the cream in a separate bowl until it forms soft peaks. Very gently fold the cream into the cheese mixture, pour the mixture into the cake pan and chill for 4–6 hours, or until firm.

For the topping, melt the broken-up chocolate in a bowl set over a pan of simmering water. Place in a small piping bag fitted with a fine nozzle (see Notes) and scribble it all over the top of the cheesecake. Refrigerate for another 30 minutes, or until the chocolate has set. Carefully release the cake from the pan (p. 159), slice into portions and serve with some extra toasted hazelnuts.

Makes one 24-cm cake; serves 8.

Notes

When you cut the cheesecake, use a knife heated over a flame to slice through the chocolate scribbles, then switch to a cool knife to cut through the rest. If you don't have a piping bag, use a large syringe, or dribble the chocolate over the top with a teaspoon.

Mango and Coconut Parfait

This rich and creamy frozen dessert is also versatile, as you can use any tropical fruit that tastes good with coconut: try it with passion fruit or sweet pineapple. Set this in a loaf pan as a parfait, or pile generous scoops into cones.

1 x 400 ml tin coconut milk
1½ cups (375 ml) fresh cream
7 extra-large free-range egg yolks
2 Tbsp (30 ml) caster sugar
1 cup (250 ml) or 1 x 385 g tin
condensed milk
3 ripe mangos
a little lemon juice

Put the coconut milk into a saucepan and whisk it to smooth out any coagulated lumps. Add the cream, set over a medium-low heat and bring slowly and gently to the boil, stirring gently now and then. When the mixture begins to seethe and rise in the pan, remove from the heat.

In the meantime, put the egg yolks and sugar into a large metal mixing bowl and whisk, using an electric beater, for 3–4 minutes, or until the mixture is pale and thick. Trickle the hot cream mixture (you may need another pair of hands for this) onto the eggs, whisking as you do so. Set the bowl over a pan of simmering water (it should fit snugly, and its base must not touch the water) and cook the custard, stirring constantly, for 3–5 minutes, or until it is hot and thick enough to coat the back of a wooden spoon. Don't allow the mixture to overheat, or it may curdle; if you have a cooking thermometer, take it to about 73 °C.

Remove the bowl from the heat, whisk in the condensed milk and set aside to cool for 15 minutes. Peel and slice the mangos and whizz to a fine purée. Fold three-quarters of the purée into the custard and stir well. Add a squeeze of lemon juice: just enough to sharpen the custard slightly. Pour the mixture into a large loaf pan lined with clingfilm (p. 156), or put it into a shallow, lidded plastic container. Pour the remaining mango purée over the top and, using a spatula, stir gently to 'ripple' it through the mixture. Cover and freeze for 8 hours, or overnight.

Invert the pan on a chilled serving platter to unmould the dessert and peel off the clingfilm. Cut into thick slices using a hot knife and serve on cold plates. If you're presenting this in cones, use a scoop dipped in hot water to form balls.

Serves 8.

Notes

Take the parfait out of the fridge about 10 minutes before serving, or it will be too hard to cut neatly. To ring the changes, stir some finely chopped mango pieces into the mixture just before you add the 'ripple'.

Hot Pears en Papillote with Chocolate and Vanilla

I love food baked in a rustling parcel because opening one up is like unwrapping a present. And these paper-wrapped pears certainly smell like Christmas when you unfurl them. This is a really easy, quick recipe that can be prepared well in advance – even the day before.

1 lemon
8 firm, just-ripe pears
150 g dark chocolate (75% cocoa solids)
8 tsp (40 ml/40 g) soft butter
8 tsp (40 ml) white sugar, plus extra for dusting
8 vanilla pods (or 4 pods, split horizontally in two; see Notes)
whipped cream or custard, for serving

If you're going to bake these right away, heat the oven to 170 °C. Cut out eight circles of baking paper, each one large enough to enclose the pears completely (see Notes). Fill a large bowl with cold water and add the juice of ½ lemon. Thinly peel the pears using a potato peeler and drop them, as you finish peeling each one, into the lemony water. When all the pears are peeled, use an apple corer to remove the cores and stalks. Trim the base of each pear so it stands upright. Put the pears back into the water to prevent them from turning brown.

Put a circle of baking paper on the counter and stand a pear (patted dry with kitchen paper) on it. Into the cavity place, in this order, two or three squares of chocolate broken into small pieces, a teaspoon of butter and a teaspoon of sugar (or less, to taste). Push a vanilla pod into the cavity, allowing its end to protrude like a pear stalk. Sprinkle a little lemon juice over the outside of the pear and dust with some extra sugar. Gather up the edges of the circle to form a parcel and secure with a length of damp raffia or string tied just above the top of the pear. Tie a neat bow on each parcel so your guests can unravel the raffia easily. Repeat with the remaining pears.

Leave the pears to stand for 45 minutes. This isn't essential, but it will give the sugar time to dissolve on the surface of the pear. (At this point, you can put the parcels in the fridge and leave them there for up to 8 hours.) Place the pears on a baking sheet and bake at 170 °C for 40–45 minutes, or until they are very soft but not collapsed. Place each parcel, still wrapped, in a shallow bowl and serve immediately with whipped cream or custard.

Serves 8.

Notes

Use unblemished, firm (but not rock-hard) pears for this dish. If you can't afford a vanilla pod per pear, scrape the seeds out of two split pods and mix them with the butter before you stuff the pears. You can recycle the vanilla pods by drying them on a sunny windowsill and then burying them in a jar of caster sugar for future cakes and bakes. The best way to cut out the paper circles is to put a large dinner plate face-down on the paper (with a chopping board underneath) and cut swiftly around it with a sharp craft knife.

Chilled Watermelon with Lemongrass and Earl Grey Tea

A cold, crisp ending to a summer meal, and good for serving after a rib-sticker of a main course. This is excellent made with fresh lemon balm or lemon verbena leaves, but as these aren't readily available in shops, I suggest you use lemongrass, with Earl Grey tea adding a lovely note of bergamot.

2½ cups (625 ml) water
⅔ cup (160 ml) white sugar
2 thumb-length strips lemon peel, white pith removed
2 stalks lemongrass
1 Earl Grey teabag
1 medium-sized seedless watermelon
lemon juice, to taste

First make a sugar syrup. Put the water and sugar into a pan and add the lemon peel. Bring to the boil, stirring occasionally, and simmer until all the sugar crystals have dissolved. Remove from the heat and cool for 5 minutes. Peel the tough outer leaves from the lemongrass, discard them, and cut the thicker, pale ends of the stalks into slices. Add these to the hot syrup along with the teabag. (If you're using lemon balm or lemon verbena, add a generous handful of leaves.) Leave the teabag in the syrup for a few minutes, or until the syrup is perfumed with tea and a light copper colour, then discard it. Chill the syrup for 6 hours, or overnight, so the lemongrass flavours can infuse.

Strain the syrup through a fine sieve into a bowl. Halve the watermelon and use a melon-baller to scoop out neat little spheres (see Notes). Put the melon balls, and 3 Tbsp (45 ml) of their juice, into the cold syrup. Set aside to steep for an hour or two. Just before you serve it, add a squeeze of lemon juice; just enough to give the syrup a pleasant acidity. Serve in pretty glasses, decorated with lemon balm, if you have it. (Avoid using fresh mint, as its taste will overwhelm the delicate watermelon flavour.) You could add a dollop of sweetened Greek yoghurt to this, but I think it's perfect as it is.

Serves 8–12, depending on the size of your serving glasses.

Notes

You can make the syrup well in advance, but add the watermelon balls no more than two hours ahead, or they will lose their crispness. If you don't have a melon-baller, use a bowl-shaped metal one-teaspoon measuring spoon, or cut the melon into neat cubes.

Black Fruit Salad with Brown-Sugar Crème Fraîche

Many pudding devotees wouldn't consider a fruit salad to be a thrilling end to a meal, but this mixture of jewel-like dark fruits, with its crunchy topping of tangy crème fraîche, is sure to win them over.

2 bunches sweet black grapes, halved and deseeded
1 cup (250 ml) blackberries
1 cup (250 ml) blueberries
1 x 425 g tin pitted black cherries, drained
6 dark plums, pitted and cut into crescents
6 ripe purple figs, quartered (optional)
½ cup (125 ml) frozen blackcurrants, thawed (optional)
3 Tbsp (45 ml) icing sugar
juice of 1 small lemon

FOR THE TOPPING
1 cup (250 ml) or 1 x 250 g tub crème fraîche or mascarpone
½ tsp (2.5 ml) vanilla extract
4 Tbsp (60 ml) light brown sugar, or more, to taste

Put all the prepared fruit into a deep, non-metallic bowl, sprinkle over the icing sugar and lemon juice and stir gently to combine. Cover the bowl with clingfilm, place in the fridge and chill for at least 30 minutes (but no longer than 2 hours).

When you're ready to serve the fruit salad, tip the crème fraîche or mascarpone into a small bowl, add the vanilla extract and brown sugar and whisk gently until smooth.

Remove the fruit salad from the fridge, stir it gently to distribute the juices, and pile it into eight chilled bowls (or onto one large platter). Top each bowl with a big dollop of crème fraîche and serve immediately.

Serves 8.

Notes

Mix the brown sugar with the crème fraîche just before you serve the salad, so it retains a pleasant crunch. If you make the topping too far in advance, the sugar will dissolve into the cream. Try ringing the changes by creating an all-red fruit salad with strawberries, raspberries, red plums, watermelon and pomegranate seeds.

Passion Fruit, Crème Fraîche and White Chocolate Tart

I am infatuated with the heady sharp-sweet taste of passion fruit, but find them quite intense, so they are used sparingly in this tart. Because I prefer a soft, voluptuous tart, I avoid cream cheese and instead use thick, slightly sour crème fraîche.

FOR THE BISCUIT CRUST
1 x 200 g packet Tennis biscuits or similar crumbly coconut biscuits
6 Tbsp (90 ml/90 g) very soft butter

FOR THE FILLING
1 x 200 g slab white chocolate, broken into small pieces
4 tsp (20 ml) tepid water
2 tsp (10 ml) powdered gelatine
1 x 250 g tub crème fraîche
½ cup (125 ml) fresh passion fruit pulp
½ cup (125 ml) condensed milk
finely grated zest of ½ lemon
4 tsp (20 ml) fresh lemon juice
1 cup (250 ml) or 1 x 250 ml tub fresh cream

FOR THE TOPPING
3 Tbsp (45 ml) fresh passion fruit pulp

Break up the biscuits and whizz them to fairly fine crumbs in a food processor. Place in a bowl, add the soft butter and stir well to combine. Line the base of a non-stick 24-cm springform cake pan with clingfilm (p. 156).

Put the white chocolate pieces in a metal bowl and place it over a pot of simmering water (it should fit snugly, and its base must not touch the water). Let the chocolate melt slowly, stirring gently now and then, but take care not to let the water boil too fast, or its steam will make the chocolate 'seize' to a claggy mixture that cannot be rescued.

Put the water in a little bowl or teacup, sprinkle the gelatine evenly on top and set aside to sponge for 5 minutes. Combine the crème fraîche, passion fruit pulp, condensed milk, lemon zest and juice in a big mixing bowl and whisk until smooth. Stir the white chocolate gently, and when it's just melted, scrape it into the mixing bowl (work quickly here, or it will set). Whisk until smooth.

Melt the sponged gelatine (p. 160), allow to cool for a few minutes, strain it into the crème fraîche mixture and stir well. In a separate bowl, whip the cream to a firm peak. Very gently fold the cream into the mixing bowl. Pile the mixture into the middle of the prepared crust, then very gently press down on the middle of the filling with the back of a big spoon so it spreads evenly outwards to 'kiss' the edges of the pan. Now lightly swirl the spoon across the top of the filling to form generous waves and ripples. Cover and chill for 3–4 hours, or until set.

Gently release the pie from its pan using a hot kitchen cloth (p. 159) and loosen its base with a palette knife or metal spatula (p. 156). Slide onto a chilled plate and drizzle the fresh passion fruit pulp on top. Serve cold.

Makes one 24-cm tart; serves 8.

Notes

When you're making a biscuit and butter crumb crust, press it quite gently onto the base of the cake pan, or it will form a base that's unpleasantly dense. A good way to achieve a flat, even, sharp-edged base is to lay a small shot glass on its side, rim touching the side of the pan, and roll it lightly round in a circle.

Baked Camembert with Fruit Mincemeat

This unusual dish is neither a dessert nor a cheese course, but something in between. It's ridiculously quick and easy to make, and makes a splendid ending to a Christmas feast.

2 just-ripe medium-sized Camembert cheeses
⅔ cup (160 ml) good-quality fruit mincemeat, from a jar
6 Tbsp (90 ml) dry white wine
finely grated zest of 1 small orange
a pinch of red chilli flakes (optional; see Notes)
very fine shreds of orange zest, for topping

Heat the oven to 180 °C. Place the cheeses in two small, pretty ovenproof dishes. Put the fruit mincemeat in a saucepan and stir in the wine, orange zest and chilli flakes. Bring to a gentle simmer and cook for 2–3 minutes, stirring occasionally.

Pour the mixture over the cheeses and place in the oven. Bake, uncovered, for 4–5 minutes, or until the cheeses are beginning to collapse and are hot and oozing. Scatter the orange zest over the top and take straight to the table with a plate of salty biscuits or cream crackers and, if you like, a plate of chilled grapes, or fresh orange or naartjie segments.

Serves 8.

Notes	To prepare ahead, simmer the mincemeat with its flavourings, allow the sauce to cool completely and pour it over the cold cheeses, ready for baking. You can leave the chilli flakes out of the sauce if you like, but I find they add an irresistible sparkle.

Figs with Hot Brie and Spicy Caramel Walnuts

This is such a versatile dish because it can be served, like the recipe on the previous page, as a combination dessert and cheese course, or as a starter or snack right at the beginning of a meal. You can also use pecans or macadamias here, but I like walnuts because their slight bitterness contrasts so well with ripe, sweet figs.

8 large, ripe figs
1 x 120 g wedge Brie, ripe but not oozing

FOR THE CARAMEL NUTS
24 shelled walnuts
5 Tbsp (75 ml) white sugar
1 tsp (5 ml) paprika
½ tsp (2.5 ml) cayenne pepper (or more, to taste)
flaky sea salt

Toast the walnuts in a dry frying pan over a medium heat, for a minute or two, until just beginning to turn golden at the edges. Set aside. Sprinkle the sugar into the saucepan and watch it closely as it begins to liquefy and turn golden in patches. Swirl the pan gently to distribute the melted patches, but don't stir. As soon as all the sugar has melted, and the caramel is a light copper colour, remove from the heat (it will continue to darken after you've removed it). Add the walnuts and toss well to coat. Fish the nuts out of the pan using a pair of tongs, put them on a plate covered with oiled baking paper and sprinkle with paprika, cayenne pepper and plenty of salt. Leave to harden, and then chop or break the nuts into big pieces.

Heat your oven's grill to its hottest setting. Put the figs into a shallow ovenproof dish. Cut a cross in the top of each fig, right through its stalk, stopping a little short of its base. Squeeze the bottoms of the figs so that the four 'petals' open up. Lightly press a wedge of cheese (how much is up to you) into each fig. Place under the hot grill, on a rack in the middle of the oven, for a few minutes, or until the cheese has melted. Remove from the oven, sprinkle over the caramelised walnuts and serve immediately with crackers and/or some iced grapes.

Serves 8.

Notes

Prepare and stuff the figs ready for grilling a few hours ahead and keep covered with clingfilm. Make the caramel walnuts a few hours ahead, allow to harden and cool completely, and store in a lidded container.

Irish Coffee Baked Alaska with a Chocolate Brownie Base

The inspiration for this recipe came to me in the middle of the night, a time when many good ideas are afoot, and it has become my family's favourite dessert. Wreathed in blue flames of whiskey, this makes a spectacular finale to a feast.

FOR THE ICE-CREAM LAYER
1.5 litres full-cream vanilla ice cream
1 cup (250 ml) or 1 x 250 ml tub fresh cream
2 Tbsp (30 ml) top-quality instant coffee granules
3 Tbsp (45 ml) whiskey, or more, to taste (see Notes)

FOR THE BROWNIE BASE
100 g butter, cubed
75 g dark chocolate (75% cocoa solids), broken into small pieces
2 extra-large free-range eggs
1 cup (250 ml) white sugar
7 Tbsp (105 ml) cake flour
2 Tbsp (30 ml) instant coffee granules
a pinch of salt
1 tsp (5 ml) baking powder

FOR THE MERINGUE
6 extra-large free-range egg whites, at room temperature
a pinch of salt
1 cup (250 ml) light brown sugar
½ cup (125 ml) whiskey, for flaming

Prepare two non-stick spring-form cake pans of the same size. Line the base of one with clingfilm (p. 156) and place in the freezer. Line the base of the second pan with a circle of greased baking paper. Take the ice cream out of the freezer and let it soften for 15 minutes. Whisk the cream to a soft peak in a mixing bowl, then beat in the coffee and whiskey. Fold in the softened ice cream, working quickly so the mixture doesn't liquefy. Tip into the clingfilm-lined pan and freeze until solid.

To make the base, heat the oven to 180 °C. Melt the butter and chocolate in a metal bowl set over a pan of simmering water (p. 159), stirring occasionally. Remove the bowl from the heat and add the eggs, sugar, flour, coffee, salt and baking powder, all in one go. Beat for 1 minute until smooth, then tip the mixture into the paper-lined pan and bake for 25–30 minutes, or until just firm to the touch. Run the tip of a knife around the edges and cool for 10 minutes. Turn onto a rack and peel off the paper. Place on an ovenproof plate and refrigerate.

About 30 minutes before you're ready to serve, release the ice cream from its mould. Position it, top-side down, on top of the brownie cake, then peel off the clingfilm. Put the cake back in the freezer. Fifteen minutes before pudding time, set the oven to 190 °C. Whisk the egg whites with the salt to a soft peak, then add the sugar, bit by bit, and beat continuously for 4–5 minutes, until you have a very firm, fluffy meringue. Spread the meringue in a thick, swirly layer all over the Alaska, taking it right to the base and making sure there are no gaps or holes. Bake for 5–6 minutes, or until the meringue is a light toasty colour.

Take the Alaska to the table and switch off the lights. Put the whiskey into a soup ladle and hold it over a flame until it is very hot. It will ignite on its own when it reaches the right temperature, or you can tilt it so it catches fire. Pour the flaming whiskey over the cake – stand well back – and, as soon as the flames die down, cut into wedges and serve.

Serves 8–10.

Notes

Don't add too much whiskey to the ice cream, as alcohol can inhibit freezing. Peel the paper off the brownie layer while it's still warm, or it will stick.

Frozen Fruit Popsicles

Light, fruity popsicles so cold they're wreathed in icy smoke cause a minor sensation at a feast, especially if it's a scorching day and there are children at the table. These are so easy to prepare, and can be made a day ahead. Each of these recipes makes enough small popsicles for eight people, so you might want to halve the quantities if you're making more than one type of popsicle.

STRAWBERRY AND BUTTERMILK POPSICLES

36 ripe, sweet strawberries, hulled and coarsely chopped
2–4 Tbsp (30–60 ml) icing sugar
a little lemon juice, to taste
1 cup (250 ml) thick cultured buttermilk, chilled

SPICED GUAVA POPSICLES

6 ripe guavas, topped and tailed, and quartered
4 Tbsp (60 ml) sugar, to taste
1 star anise
1 x 5-cm stick of cinnamon
1 strip of fresh lemon peel, white pith removed
2 tsp (10 ml) lemon juice
1 cup (250 ml) fresh cream or thick natural yoghurt

PASSION FRUIT AND LEMON CREAM POPSICLES

8 large ripe passion fruits
½ cup (125 ml) condensed milk
finely grated zest and juice of 1 small lemon
½ cup (125 ml) fresh cream, lightly whipped

STRAWBERRY AND BUTTERMILK POPSICLES

Put the strawberries into a metal bowl and add some icing sugar and lemon juice. How much depends on the sweetness of the strawberries; if they're very sweet, add just a dusting of icing sugar and a squeeze of lemon for acidity. Stir and set aside for 30 minutes. Put a quarter of this mixture in the fridge; this will form the tops of the popsicles. Freeze the remaining strawberries for 4–6 hours, or until frozen solid. Put a blob of the reserved strawberries in the bottom of eight or more small glasses (see Notes). Pour the cold buttermilk over the frozen strawberries and let the mixture stand for 5 minutes. Scrape the still-frozen mixture into a food processor. Whizz to a thick purée. Divide the mixture between the glasses, push a wooden stick deep into the middle of each glass and return to the freezer. To unmould the popsicles, warm the glasses with a wet cloth you've heated in the microwave (p. 159). Serve the popsicles on a bed of crushed ice.

SPICED GUAVA POPSICLES

Place the guavas in a saucepan and add the sugar (to taste), star anise, cinnamon and lemon peel. Add just enough water to cover the guavas, bring to a gentle boil and simmer for 8 minutes, or until the guavas are just soft. Stir in the lemon juice and set aside to infuse for a few hours. Fish the guavas from their syrup (save the spiced syrup for future desserts), chop them roughly and put a quarter of this mixture in the fridge. Freeze the remaining guavas and continue with the recipe, as described above, using cream or thick natural yoghurt instead of buttermilk.

PASSION FRUIT AND LEMON CREAM POPSICLES

Halve the passion fruits and scoop out the pulp. Set aside. Whip the condensed milk, lemon zest and lemon juice until smooth and slightly thickened (p. 163), then fold in the whipped cream and passion fruit pulp. Set the mixture aside to thicken for 15 minutes, then spoon into popsicle moulds, as described above. Push the sticks into the moulds and freeze until hard.

Notes

Shot glasses or tiny yoghurt tubs make ideal moulds for popsicles, or you can use plastic lolly moulds. Keep the popsicles well covered so they don't pick up freezer odours, and make them no more than two days ahead. Ring the changes by experimenting with other perfumed fruits, such as summer berries, oranges, pineapples and mangos.

Basic Recipes

Vinaigrette

The classic proportion of acid to oil in a vinaigrette is one part vinegar (or lemon juice) to three parts oil. I tend to prefer lemony dressings because I find many vinegars, and especially the ubiquitous balsamic vinegar, too aggressive for delicate salads.

4 Tbsp (60 ml) vinegar or lemon juice, or a combination (see Notes)
½ tsp (2.5 ml) Dijon or similar mustard
a pinch each of flaky sea salt and white sugar
¾ cup (180 ml) extra-virgin olive, sunflower or canola oil, or a combination
milled black pepper

Put the vinegar (or lemon juice), mustard, salt and sugar in a bowl and stir to dissolve the sugar and salt. Slowly whisk in the oil to form a smooth emulsion. Season with pepper and more salt, to taste. If the mixture is too thick, whisk in 1 tsp (5 ml) of warm water. Add any flavourings you fancy – garlic, or fresh or dried herbs, honey, wholegrain mustard, fresh orange juice, chillies, and so on.

Makes about 1 cup (250 ml) dressing.

Notes | Don't leave the mustard out; it helps the vinaigrette emulsify. You can use any good-quality vinegar or stick to fresh lemon or lime juice. Or you can go for a combination of vinegar and citrus juice. I use half-and-half olive oil and sunflower (or canola) oil. Often I add a few drops of Kikkoman soy sauce as I find it magically brings all the flavours together.

Mayonnaise

It is possible to make a quick homemade mayonnaise in a blender, but the problem with this method is that you can't keep an eye on the consistency of the mixture, so I use an electric beater or, if I have time, I whisk it by hand. Mayonnaise really isn't difficult to make, but do take your time over it. Make it calmly and patiently in a quiet kitchen, measure everything precisely, and you won't go wrong.

2 extra-large free-range egg yolks, at room temperature
a pinch of flaky sea salt
½ tsp (2.5 ml) Dijon or similar mustard
200 ml sunflower oil
100 ml extra-virgin olive oil
2 Tbsp (30 ml) lemon juice or vinegar
milled black pepper
1 tsp (5 ml) warm water

Put the egg yolks, salt and mustard into a bowl. Using an electric beater, whisk the yolks until creamy. Mix the oils in a jug. Turn the beater to its highest speed. Now, as you whisk the egg yolks with one hand, dribble the oil onto the yolks, just a few drops at a time, with the other. Continue whisking and dribbling on the oil, and within a few minutes you will see the mixture begin to thicken dramatically. Keep adding oil in a steady trickle until you have a thick, pale yellow ointment. Stir in enough lemon juice or vinegar to sharpen the mayonnaise to your liking. Season with salt and pepper, then stir in the warm water. Now stir in any additional ingredients: garlic, lemon zest, fresh herbs, anchovies, and so on.

Makes about 300 ml mayonnaise.

Chicken Stock

A good homemade stock, with its many intermingled layers of flavour, will elevate a savoury dish from merely tasty to quite delicious. Mine is not the fine, pellucid stock used by professional chefs for consommés, but a golden, flavoursome broth that adds lovely depth to soups, sauces, pies and casseroles. You can use just a single whole chicken, but adding wings (or thighs, or an additional fresh chicken carcass) to the pot will provide the collagen necessary to create a really excellent stock (and by that I mean one that, when chilled, turns to a rich, wobbling jelly).

1 large free-range chicken, trimmed of excess fat
8 chicken wings or 6 thighs, or a fresh chicken carcass (optional)
3 litres water, or enough to cover the chicken to a depth of 7 cm
1 cup (250 ml) white wine (optional)
1½ tsp (7.5 ml) sea salt
1 large onion, skin on, quartered
2 leeks, trimmed, rinsed and sliced
3 large carrots, peeled and roughly chopped
2 stalks celery, thickly sliced
6 stalks flat-leaf parsley
3 sprigs fresh thyme
3 whole cloves
2 bay leaves
1 tsp (5 ml) black peppercorns

Place the whole chicken and the wings (or thighs, or extra carcass) in a stock pot and add the water, wine and salt. Bring gently to the boil, then turn down the heat and simmer for 10 minutes. Skim off all the foam as it rises. Now add all the remaining stock ingredients and bring back up to the boil. Cover with a tilted lid, turn down the heat and simmer very gently – the water should remain at a calm burble – for 2 hours, topping up with more water if necessary. Let the stock cool to lukewarm, then strain it into a clean bowl through a sieve lined with a fine cloth (a laundered napkin or a brand-new kitchen cloth is ideal). Discard the solids. Refrigerate until quite cold, then lift off the congealed fat. If you'd like a really intense-tasting stock, put the pot back on the stove and simmer, uncovered, until the liquid has reduced by half. Store, covered, in the fridge for up to 3 days, or freeze in lidded plastic containers or clingfilm-covered ice trays for up to 3 months.

Makes about 2 litres of stock.

Notes

If you would like to use some of the cooked chicken breasts for sandwiches, remove the whole chicken from the stock after about 35 minutes, cut away the breasts, then put the chicken back into the pot. Breasts simmered for the entire 2 hours are inedible.

Another way to create a really deep-flavoured stock (and tender poached chicken to use in another dish) is to simmer a carcass and wings for 2 hours, as described in the recipe, then add a whole, new chicken, and let that simmer for another hour, or until cooked through.

For an extra-rich stock, you can lightly fry all the vegetables, herbs, spices and carcass bones in a mixture of hot olive oil and butter before you add the water and whole chicken. For warm colour, add a few roughly chopped tomatoes.

A good way to clarify and de-fat a stock is to use chef Heston Blumenthal's method: freeze the stock in a round bowl, then place it in a big sieve or colander lined with several layers of kitchen paper. Set the sieve over a large bowl. As the stock thaws and drips into the bowl, the fat and impurities stay behind on the paper.

Béchamel Sauce

Here's how to make a classic béchamel or white sauce. If you've turned to this page to find out how to make the sauce for a particular recipe, please disregard the quantities below and use the exact amount of flour, butter and milk specified in the recipe you're following.

4 Tbsp (60 ml/60 g) butter
4 Tbsp (60 ml) cake flour
2 cups (500 ml) cold milk (see Notes)
salt and pepper

Melt the butter in a saucepan over a medium heat, then stir in the flour to make a roux. Let the butter and flour sizzle for about a minute and a half, and keep stirring, but don't allow the flour or butter to brown. Pour in the milk, all in one go, and, using a balloon whisk, beat the mixture with great energy to break up any floury lumps. Alternatively, you can add the milk in small increments, whisking as you go. Cook, stirring constantly, until the sauce is smooth and thick. Let the sauce bubble gently for a further 4–5 minutes, then stir in any other ingredients specified in the recipe: cheese, mustard, lemon juice, cream, chopped parsley, and so on. Season to taste with salt and pepper.

Makes about 2 cups (500 ml) sauce.

Notes

Infusing the milk with some aromatics before it's added to the sauce helps create a more complex flavour. Pour the milk into a saucepan and add ½ onion, 1 bay leaf, 1 blade of mace (optional), a few stalks of parsley and 10 whole peppercorns. Place over a low heat and bring very gently up to a slow simmer; this should take at least 5 minutes. Turn off the heat, cover the surface of the milk with a sheet of clingfilm and allow to cool. Now strain the milk into a clean jug.

Whether you add the milk to the roux in one go or bit by bit is up to you. I find that cold milk added all at once and diligently whisked as it thickens produces the best result. An advantage of adding the milk a little at a time, on the other hand, is that you can stop adding it once the sauce has thickened to your liking.

If you'd like a very smooth and shiny sauce, strain it through a fine sieve before you add any other ingredients.

Recipe Index

Page numbers in **bold** indicate photographs.